# BLACK HISTORY THROUGH BLUE EYES

## JAMES J. SEYMOUR

*THE DEBT THE WORLD OWES TO AFRICA*

# BLACK HISTORY THROUGH BLUE EYES:

# THE DEBT THE WORLD OWES TO AFRICA

By

James J. Seymour



Library of Congress Control Number:  00-93683

ISBN: 978-0-9710067-0-6

Additional copies of this book are available by mail.  Send $15.00 donation for each copy to:
First Steps Ministries, Inc.
6604 Glendower Road
Raleigh, North Carolina 27613

Printed in the United States by:
Morris Publishing
3212 East Highway 30
Kearney, NE  68847
1-800-650-7888

Cover Photography
Copyright © 2000 by
Morris Press

# DEDICATION

This book is dedicated to my wife Dawn, my partner in ministry and mother to our three wonderful children, Jessica, Aaron and Heather; proud mother-in-law to Brian Johnson and Aaron Santmyire, and devoted grandmother to our Isaac.

## ACKNOWLEDGEMENTS

I will be eternally grateful to my students and colleagues in Zimbabwe, Africa who honored me with your friendship and allowing me to learn and grow with you for twelve years and who have continued to treat me as your brother. Also to my students and colleagues at Saint Augustine's College in Raleigh, North Carolina, who have shared your lives as well as your expertise with me while working on this project. I want to specifically thank those who donated many hours in proof-reading and feedback, namely Dr. Alisea C. McCleod, Dr. Anthony Grady, Dr. Lalchand Shimpi, Dr. Frederick C. Jones, Mr. Don Donaldson, and Miss Xiamara Shepherd. I want to give an added thanks to my wife Dawn for countless hours at the computer making corrections on the manuscript. Finally, my gratitude to the late architect and my friend Cy McGee and his wife Rose Ann, whose investment in this project made publication possible.

## ABOUT THE AUTHOR

James J. Seymour holds a Doctor of Ministry Degree and a Masters of Divinity Degree from Faith Evangelical Lutheran Seminary. He has also earned a Masters Degree in Community/Agency Counseling from Fairfield University, a Bachelors Degree in Secondary Education, History from Southeastern College, and a Ministerial Diploma from Zion Bible Institute.

# TABLE OF CONTENTS


Introduction:     Do I Have The Right To Write? 5

Chapter 1     The Location of Eden....................7

Chapter 2     Where Did Racial Prejudice
Come From? ...................................12

Chapter 3     Thank God For Egypt.................23

Chapter 4     Old Testament African
Heroes .......................................31

Chapter 5     The Family Tree of Jesus..............42

Chapter 6     Black Ministers in the New
Testament...................................50

Chapter 7     Early Church Fathers From
Africa.........................................60

Chapter 8     African-American Religious
Pioneers......................................70

Chapter 9     The Untold Story of Black
Missionaries...................................88

Chapter 10     The Neglect of Samaria ...............97

Chapter 11     One Brick at a Time....................114

# INTRODUCTION

## MY RIGHT TO WRITE

The question might well be asked, what right do I have as a white male to write about Black History?  It is a valid question.  I am not intending to project myself as an expert in the field of Black Studies as there are many outstanding scholars among us who have dedicated their lives to this area of focus.

My perspective is more experiential than theoretical.  I spent twelve years living on the continent of Africa in the nation of Zimbabwe.  I arrived there at the very beginning of 1980 during the days of the cease-fire in the Liberation War.  Since 1965 Rhodesia had been under sanctions from the United Nations for her refusal to allow a democratic form of government in this former British Colony.

The Rhodesian Prime Minister Ian Smith had boldly declared when asked about allowing the black population to vote: "never in a thousand years."  After seven years of intense warfare, the troops of Robert Mugabe and Joshua Nkomo, forced a negotiated settlement at the Lancaster House in London, and the war came to an end.  In April of 1980, Robert Mugabe was elected Prime Minister of the new nation called Zimbabwe.

For twelve years my wife and three children enjoyed the privilege of learning, serving, and growing together with the people of Zimbabwe.  I was primarily involved in Theological Education and as the director of a Counseling Center.  My entire family grew to love and respect the people of Africa.  Surely I learned more from the people than I ever taught them.  I watched their courage to endure during times of drought and shortages.  I observed their cheerful attitudes, even with few material possessions.  I was moved by the commitment to the extended family, and I was touched by the grace of forgiveness extended to their former oppressors.

My present position also affords me a wonderful experiential education.  As Head of the Department of Religion and Philosophy at Saint Augustine's College in Raleigh, North Carolina I enjoy a most fulfilling life.  This school is one of the 116 Historically Black Colleges and Universities in America.  It was founded in 1867 by the Protestant Episcopal Church to train former slaves as schoolteachers and ministers.  It has a glorious history, and distinguished alumni.  I feel honored to be a part of its present contribution to offering education to students from various parts of America, as well as other nations.  Every day my life is enriched, and I am changed as I interact with the faculty and student body of this College.

Do I have the right to write?  Absolutely not.  I have the privilege to write about a courageous and often mistreated people, for whose contribution the world owes an incredible debt.  The salvation history of the Bible would not be possible without the people of Africa.  Great men and women who can trace their ancestral roots to the continent of Africa have also overwhelmingly impacted the development of the Christian Church in America.

Let me hasten to say that I am borrowing heavily on the research of a number of fine authors who have been studying this vast topic for many years, but in certain segments of the population their research has never been read.  This is largely a work of secondary research not primary research and I will clearly and gladly give credit to all my sources.

My focus audience in writing this book is primarily my brothers and sisters in Christ from the white Christian community who are largely uninformed about the prominent role of the people of Africa in the development of the Bible as well as of the incredible contribution of the African-American community in the spread of Christianity across America.

# CHAPTER 1

## THE LOCATION OF EDEN

Many of us have had the opportunity to see a variety of movies and videos with a Biblical theme produced over the years. I have seen several that depict the Biblical story of creation as found in Genesis chapters 1-2. The thing that amazes me is that in every one of these films when the man is created from the dust of the earth he always turns out to be white and so does the woman who is created soon thereafter. What is it that we need to know here?

To begin we need to do some Biblical investigation and ask the question - where exactly was the Garden of Eden where the first man was created? Three basic facts must be considered. First, we must consider the maps of the ancient Bible lands. In the Bible there is not one single mention of Germany (the cradle of the Reformation) or of England (publishers of the King James Version of the Bible); by contrast, however, countries in Africa are mentioned again and again. The Old Testament alone cites Ethiopia over forty times and Egypt over one hundred times. Many Biblical and extra-Biblical sources mention Egypt and Ethiopia together, almost interchangeably.

Secondly, the Bible provides extensive evidence that the earliest people were located in Africa. The Garden of Eden account, found in Genesis 2:8-14, indicates that the first two rivers of Eden were in ancient Cush, a term that the Greeks would later transpose "Athiops" or Ethiopia meaning literally burnt face people. Genesis 2:11-12 connects the Pishion River with Havilah, a direct descendant of Cush. (Genesis 10:7) The Gihon River is cited in Genesis 2:13 as the second River in Eden surrounding the whole land of Cush.

Thirdly, the ancient land of Canaan was but an extension of the African land mass. In Biblical times, African peoples often migrated from the continent through Canaan/Palestine to the east to what was then Asia, namely the "Fertile Crescent" or the Tigris and the Euphrates Rivers of the Ancient Mesopotamia.  This fact helps us to appreciate the term Afro-Asiatic as correctly identifying the mixed stock of people who populated the Ancient Near East.  Although Europeans (Greeks and Romans) began to feature in the more recent Biblical narratives, the fact remains that the earliest Biblical people, by modern western standards of racial types, would have to be classified as blacks; they were of African descent and possessed African features[1].

## THE TALE OF FOUR RIVERS

——Ethiopia——

| HIDDEKEL | GIHON |
|---|---|
| OR | OR |
| TIGRIS RIVER | NILE RIVER |

*THE GARDEN OF EDEN*

| EUPHRATES RIVER | PISHON RIVER |
|---|---|

——Ethiopia——

Figure 1

---

[1] Cain Hope Felde, "The Original African Heritage Study Bible," (Nashville: Winston-Derek Publishers, 1992).

One of the distinguishing features of Eden was the river that passed through the region to nourish the garden, then dividing into four heads. The source of this great river originated from beneath the earth. According to Scripture at this time, it had not yet begun to rain on the earth and would not until the days of Noah. (Gen. 2:5-6: 7:4,12-13)

The mighty river of Eden played a profound role in bringing forth the world's first established nation, Ethiopia (Gen. 2:11,13). The Byzantium, Stephanus, while commenting on the universal ancient world, spoke of Ethiopia as *the first country on earth.* The ancient historians spoke of the Ethiopians as *the first people to have ever lived.* The African-Ethiopians called themselves *Autochthones,* meaning, "sprung from the soil they inhabited." (Gen. 2:10)

The first river to depart from the gigantic river of Eden was the Pishon. (Gen. 2:11) This huge river circled the whole land of Havilah, which contained gold, bdellium and onyx stone, and gushed northwest of Ethiopia, merging with the Gihon River. The Jewish historian Genzgerg says, the Pishon, while flowing from Eden, poured silver and gold into the Nile. He makes reference to Adam and Noah's association with the Pishon river, and that this river existed in Southern Ethiopia. The Jewish professors Yohanan Aharoni and Michael Aiv-Yonah, in their book *The Macmillan Bible Atlas,* illustrate the Pishon as the *Blue Nile* flowing down the highlands of Ethiopia.

The Roman historian Pliny spoke of a Havilah in East Africa. Pliny also described bdellium, one of Havilah's precious substances, as black in color. (Pliny, EP vi 28, xii 36) The 1904 *Encyclopedia Britannica* spoke of an African bdellium along the Eastern coast of Africa, and that bdellium possessed a dark-red color. This fragrance is also mentioned in the 1914 *Century Dictionary and Cyclopedia* as existing in Southern Egypt. In the legends of the Jews, bdellium is linked with Eden, Ethiopia and Egypt. The African Havilah mentioned by Windsor, Pliny, Aharoni, and Avi-Yonah is the same Havilah that Moses spoke about in Genesis 2:11-12, as producing bdellium.[2]

The name of the second river to divide from the principal river of Eden was the Gihon. (Gen. 2:13) This great river circled the whole land of Ethiopia, and then headed north of Ham (known today as Africa, Psalm 78:51; 105: 23-27; 106:19-23), spilling into the Great Sea (Mediterranean) and the Red Sea. The Jewish historian Flavius Josephus says that the Gihon River was the Nile in Africa.[3] The Greeks called the Nile the *River of Ham,* referring to the ancient son of Noah. (Gen. 6:10) The Nile, according to Webster' (1979) *Webster Encyclopedia Dictionary* and to Hastings' (1903) *Dictionary of the Bible,* is equivalent to the word Shihor (I Chron. 13:5; Jer. 2:18) meaning, "black or dark blue."

The name of the third river to flow from the great river of Africa was the *Hiddekel.* This swift, wild river, while flowing from Paradise, apparently plunged underground, flowing hundreds of miles, before resurfacing in the Fertile Crescent, thereby reverting southward, traveling toward the east of Assyria, to adjoin the Persian Gulf. The contemporary name for the Hiddekel is *Tigris,* a Persian word, meaning arrow. The Hiddekel apparently disjoined Africa largely due to the break-up of the super continent, which was triggered by certain violent changes in the earth, forcing Africa and Asia to geographically split. The new sea between its shores was called the *Red Sea.*

The name of the fourth river was the Euphrates. (Gen. 2: 14) This peaceful river's departure from the main source of Eden, and its destination, was similar to the Hiddekel's. The Jewish Philo called the Euphrates *Aracani,* while Josephus preferred *Prath.* The Greek Philostratus says the Armenians and Arabs of this epoch were convinced that the Euphrates River flowed to Africa underground, then mingled with the

---

[2] Julian Ramsses Johnson, " The Garden of Eden" ( Nashville: James C. Winston Publishing Com., 1994)

[3] W. Whinston, " The Life and Works of Flavius Josephus" (1981)

Nile.   The Egyptologist James Henry Breasted indicates that the eastern Mediterranean once flowed into the Euphrates, causing the Euphrates to spill into the Nile Delta.[4]

## SOME REASONABLE CONCLUSIONS

The main factor to note is that two very distinct land areas are identified in the naming of these rivers. Namely what we know of today as Africa, and the nearer Middle East. A little over a century ago, these two land areas were connected. The completion of the Suez Canal in 1869 introduced a man-made separation that has affected not only the land, but also its cultural and social fabric as well. World War II correspondents introduced the new name Middle East for the portion of land separated from the main African Continent. Prior to these events, much of the land was known as Northeast Africa.

We also see in Genesis that the Garden was planted "eastward in Eden."  Between the Nile and the Euphrates, meaning the whole region of which this garden was a part, was called Eden, which translated from Hebrew means "Pleasure" or "delight," in other words "paradise."  It stands to reason that if the region from which the Biblical Garden of Eden extends was then known as Northeast Africa, then we should have no trouble accepting Africa as the cradle of civilization.[5] Even today's contemporary scholars verify that the first people of the earth were of African descent.  The famous anthropologist Louis Leaky made important discoveries of the earliest and oldest fossil remains of man in eastern Africa.  I do not feel it would be presumptuous for me to say that when God made man out of the dust of the earth, and breathed into his nostrils the breath of life, *it was African dust!*

---

[4] Julian Ramsses Johnson, "The Garden of Eden" (Nashville: James C. Winston Publishing Com., 1994)

[5] Cain Hope Felder, "The Original African Heritage Study Bible" (Nashville: Winston-Derek Publishers, 1992)

# CHAPTER 2
# WHERE DID RACIAL PREJUDICE COME FROM?

## THE CONCEPT OF RACE AND COLOR

Bigotry, 'in the sense of preferring one's people to other people,' is as old as recorded history, but racism in the sense of dehumanizing others on the basis of their skin color is a modern phenomenon.  For many people, the meaning of the term *race* is simple: Different races are people of different *skin colors.* There are problems with this simple method of distinguishing races. For one, skin coloring varies enormously. There are people whose parents are of one "race" but who could easily be classified as members of a different "race," on the basis of skin color.   Furthermore, because there are so many shades of skin color, classifying a person as a member of one or another race on that basis is arbitrary.

Many anthropologists have argued that we should abandon the concept of race.  Nevertheless, people continue to identify different races primarily on the basis of skin color.[6]

## AN AMERICAN OVERVIEW OF RACE

There is actually no mention of race in the modern sense of the word until after 1492 and the advent of colonial expansionism.   Racism as a system by which one group of people has social, economic, political, and military power over another group to which it sees itself to be inherently superior due to skin pigmentation is actually a modern phenomenon. It is forever linked in American history to the Atlantic slave trade of the 16th, 17th, 18th, and 19th centuries. According to Harvard scholar Cornell West:

---

[6] Robert H. Lauer, " Social Problems and the Quality of Life," (Boston: McGraw –Hill Co., 1998), p. 318

Francois Bernier, a French physician, first employed the very category 'race,' denoting primarily skin color, as a means of classifying human bodies in 1684. The first authoritative racial division of humankind is found in the influential *Natural System* (1735) of the preeminent naturalist Carolus Linnaeus.[7]

When Christopher Columbus accidentally "discovered" the Americas, he opened up new economic opportunities for the rising nation-states of Western Europe. Spain, Portugal, France, the Netherlands, and England quickly undertook to exploit the natural and agricultural resources of this "New World." The development of gold and silver mines and sugar, coffee, tobacco, rice and cotton plantations, required a large and relatively cheap labor force.

After experimenting with enslaved Native Americans and the European poor, the colonizers began to import large numbers of African slaves, who proved to be skilled workers, resistant to many tropical diseases, and readily available. Between 1501 and 1870, nearly twelve million Africans were forcibly loaded aboard ships on the West African coast and taken to the Americas.[8]

It is essential to realize, however, that the first Africans in English America were not slaves, but arrived on the same economic terms on which many English and Irish settlers came. In August 1619, one year after the *Mayflower* landed, and over a hundred years before George Washington's birth, twenty Africans were captured from a Spanish slave ship arrived in Jamestown. Spain was already involved in the slave trade, but England was not. Two of the liberated slaves from that ship were named Anthony and Isabella. They married at

---

[7] Cornell West, " Prophetic Fragments" ( Grand Rapids, Michigan: William B. Eerdsman Publishing, 1988), p.100

[8] Roy, Finkenbine, " Sources of the African American Past" (New York: Longman Publishers USA),p.1.

Jamestown and named their son William Tucker in 1624. William Tucker was the first African-American in the modern sense, and he was not a slave.[9]

Over the next four decades, Black Americans bought land, voted, testified in court, mingled with whites on a basis of equality. Slavery already existed among some West African peoples, but Arab slave traders first introduced African slaves into Europe among the Spanish and Portuguese.

The practice in the British Colonies was called indentured servitude, which was a seven-year term of service after which a servant was to be freed and awarded land to make his own living.  This was based on an Old Testament practice meant to wean the Israelites, newly freed from slavery in Egypt, away from practicing slavery at all.

The colonists quickly learned, however, that it was more economically advantageous to exploit African servants than to exploit European ones.  If they oppressed British subjects, on the other hand, these subjects could appeal to the king for help if their term of servitude was unfairly extended. African indentured servants, however, had no one to whom they could appeal, and could not blend into the local population if they escaped, thus making their recapture relatively easy.

The consequence was the exploitation of African slave labor in the British colonies.  The basis of slavery was economic.  Racism, the dehumanization of African peoples based on their skin color, was simply an ideology created to justify economic exploitation. Once economic motives supported racism, it quickly became the law of the land, affecting primarily Africans but, by extension, all those not clearly from the continent of Europe. As Ellis Cose notes:

> Americans have always defined themselves largely on the basis of race.  The nations first citizenship statute,

---

[9]  Glenn and Keener Usery, " Black Man's Religion" ( Downers Grove: Intervaristy Press Inc. 1997)

passed in 1790, limited naturalization to 'aliens being free white persons.' The law (though amended to grant citizenship to blacks after the civil war) stood until 1952. It forced generations of nonwhite petitioners, including natives of India and Japan, to try to prove, as late as the 1940s, that they were white.[10]

## A RECENT GLOBAL PERSPECTIVE

Although the racial bigotry in America is in fact unique to its history as a nation, other people around the world also have a sad legacy of discrimination and violence based on ethnic or racial loyalties. With the fall of the Soviet Union in recent years, ancient conflicts have resurfaced in the most brutal ways. Bosnia's "ethnic cleansing" has brought about some of the most cruel violence in Europe since the days of Adolph Hitler and the Nazi's attempt at genocide against the Jews.

Conflict among the Croats and Serbs became so destructive that United Nations security forces had to intervene. South Africa's former apartheid practices have now been exposed under the leadership of Nobel prize winner Bishop Desmund Tutu. The world is horrified to hear details of torture, assassination squads, and man's inhumanity to man. The Indians of Central America have been subjected to oppression by colonial forces for generations. The caste system in India is well documented and endorsed through religious sanction to exalt certain groups in society and oppress others due to the caste in which they are born. Citizens to this country can escape only through death or the hope of a better rebirth in their next life.

Tribal genocide in Rwanda and Burundi in the late 1990's stunned the world due to the shear numbers of people killed and the unspeakably violent way in which whole families have been destroyed. A missionary from the area was quoted

---

[10] Oswald J. Sanders, " Spiritual Leadership" (Chicago: Moody Press, 1994)

in Time Magazine in October 1996 as saying, "there are no more demons left in hell...they have all moved to Rwanda."

## BIBLICAL PRINCIPLES CONCERNING RACE

## CREATION

An important question for many is simply, *what does the Bible say about race?* In reality, the Bible teaches that there is only one race, and that is the "human race." The Bible does not explicitly describe the origin of the different races of mankind. A reasonable possibility from a Biblical perspective is that when God confused and differentiated languages at Babel, He may have also made some racial or physical differentiation's as well (Genesis 11:1-9). This divinely created confusion was to divide man's rebellious unity against Him.[11] Some prophecies concerning this common ancestry are as follows:

> According to the Bible then, all of humanity comes from the very same "family tree." In both Adam and Noah, we all have common ancestry.

> Isaiah the prophet proclaimed: O Lord, you are our father. We are the clay, you are the potter; we are all the work of your hand. (Isa. 64:8)

> The prophet Malachi asks: Have we not all one Father? Did not one God create us? (Mal. 2:10)

> In the New Testament, Paul preached: From one man (one blood KJV); He made every nation of men, that they should inhabit the whole earth; and He determined the times set for them the exact places where they should live. (Acts 17:26)

---

[11]  JL, Williams, " What the Bible Teaches About Race" ( Burlington: New Directions Publishers, 1996)

Therefore, through creation, everyone belongs to the same racial group, the *human race.* Even though there is ultimately just one "family tree," there are apparently a number of "racial limbs" and "ethnic twigs" on that same tree. The tendency is to synthesize into a new branch of the family tree of nations when there are so-called "mixed races" like the Samaritan people of the Bible, the Coloreds of South Africa the Mulattos of Haiti, or the Amerasians in Vietnam.

## CORRUPTION

According to the Bible, the spiritual Fall of man (Genesis 3) from his original position of sinlessness and innocence in the Garden of Eden radically affected every area of his life, including race. As a result of man's rebellion against God, sin has manifested itself in racial conflict and confusion throughout history and all over the world. Rebellion against God seems to always result in rebellion against man. At its core, racism is a sin problem not a skin problem!

## CHRIST

Sin and the Fall has had a radically negative affect in every area of man's life. Redemption in Christ offers the possibility to radically and positively affect every area of our lives. Through the Fall, man was cast down and broken, through grace, he has been picked up and repaired! Sin confused our racial identity and unity and created insecurity, prejudice, and fear.

Racial prejudice actually is the result of self-doubt. The individual, who exemplifies and expresses any form of racial prejudice, is only demonstrating his or her own racial doubts, insecurities, and fears. This racial confusion manifests itself in the response whereby some have feelings of racial superiority and others feelings of racial inferiority. Both feelings are equally unscriptural.[12]

The Bible teaches that the cross of Jesus Christ negates all of our prejudices and fears.  Tragically, this is an area of growth that has yet to take place in the lives of many who call themselves people of faith.  This is demonstrated by the fact that Christian churches tend to meet, fellowship, and worship largely around racial, tribal, and ethnic lines.  However, all of humanity stands on equal, level ground at the foot of the cross!  No racial group is closer to the cross or to Christ than any other.  Fellowship at the foot of the cross should be demonstrated by **unity.**  Listen to the words of the Apostle Paul:

> Christ's love compels us, because we are convinced that one died for all...and He died for all, that those who live should no longer live for themselves but for Him who died for them and was raised again. So from now on, we regard no one from a worldly point of view. Though we once regarded Christ in this way, we do so no longer.  Therefore, if anyone is in Christ, he is a new creation, the old is gone, and the new has come. All this is from God, who reconciled us to Himself through Christ and gave us the ministry of reconciliation (II Cor. 5:14-18).

What Paul was saying was that, within the faith community of the Christian Church, the same racism, prejudice, bigotry and division that typifies and divides the world, should not exist. The community of believers must understand the following:

> Here there is no Greek or Jew, circumcised or uncircumcised, barbarian, Scythian, slave or free, but Christ is all, and is in all (Col. 3:11).

Paul reminded the Christians at Ephesus how Jesus had broken down the wall of prejudice dividing His people, and brought an end to the hostility that existed between the Jews and Gentiles of his day:

> ...now in Christ Jesus you who once were far away have been brought near through the blood of Christ. For He Himself is our peace, who has made the two one and has destroyed the barrier, the dividing wall of hostility...His purpose was to create in Himself one new man out of the two, thus making peace, and in this one body *to reconcile* both of them to God through the cross, by which he put to death their hostility...for through Him we both have access to the Father by one Spirit (Eph. 2:13-18).

In the same way, the wall of separation between people of different races and ethnic backgrounds today has been destroyed by the cross of Christ. It is the height of contradiction for people who say they are part of the Body of Christ, the Church, and to still live in conflict and separation from each other.

## NOAH'S THREE SONS

One theory prescribed to by some is that the races can be divided through the three sons of Noah. One must be careful to state that this is only a theory, which can lead to as many questions as it does to answers. Note what the Bible says:

> The sons of Noah who came out of the ark were Shem, Ham and Japheth. (Ham was the father of Canaan.) These were the three sons of Noah, and from them came the people who were scattered over the earth (Gen. 9: 18-19).

The theory can be summarized in the following way:

**Japheth** - means bright or fair.  He is said to be the father of the Caucasian and the Indo-European races. Moving north from Babel his descendants settled Magog, Gomer, and the regions north of the Caspian and Black Seas.

**Shem** - means dusky or olive colored.  He was the father of the Hebrew (Semitic) and Arab races. Moving south and west from Babel they settled in Biblical Assyria.  The descendants of Shem include the Jewish, Persian, Assyrian, Chaldean, Armenian and Syrian races.

**Ham** - means dark or black.  He was the father of the Black, Indian and Mongoloid races.

<table>
<tr><td colspan="3" align="center">NOAH<br><br>(Second Father<br>of Mankind)</td></tr>
<tr><td align="center"><u>SHEM</u><br>(Father of the<br>Hebrews)</td><td align="center"><u>HAM</u><br>(Father of the<br>Black Race)</td><td align="center"><u>JAPHETH</u><br>(Father of the<br>Indo-Europeans)</td></tr>
<tr><td align="center"><u>DESCENDANTS</u><br>Elam, Asshur<br>Arphaxad, Lud</td><td align="center"><u>DESCENDANTS</u><br>Cush,Mizriam<br>Phut, Canaan</td><td align="center"><u>DESCENDANTS</u><br>Gomer, Magog<br>Madai, Javan,</td></tr>
</table>

Figure 2

A valid question would be how can we believe that Noah and his wife went into the ark as a white couple, as shown in art and films portraying them, and came out with white, Black, and Asian children.  It does not make sense logically or scientifically that within the ten generations from Adam to Noah, a genetic change took place, which allowed two people of the same race to produce offspring of three different races. There is another explanation potentially, and that is that Noah and his wife were of dark genetic heritage to begin with.

Some medical research indicates that it is possible to have children that are very different, especially if one or both parents are dark complexioned. However, it is impossible for two bright or fair complexioned persons to produce a dark complexioned child. For Noah to have fathered a dark complexioned son, he or his wife had to have had dark skin. Genesis 2:7 declares, that Adam was made from the dust of the ground. Adam in Hebrew is Adahm, which means red or taken out of red earth. The name Adam also translates to man. The prefix hu means color. So it can be concluded that the human, Adam, made from the dust, was, as previously suggested, a man of color.

## THE MYTH OF THE CURSE OF HAM

Before moving on, let me finally dispel the evil and destructive myth that the Bible says that God has cursed the Black race. One close look at Scripture can once and for all time bring clarity and truth. This Biblical statement is as follows:

Noah, a man of the soil, proceeded to plant a vineyard. When he drank some of its wine, he became drunk and lay uncovered inside his tent. Ham, the father of Canaan, saw his fathers nakedness and told his two brothers outside. But Shem and Japheth took a garment and laid it across their shoulders; then they walked in backward and covered their father's nakedness. Their faces were turned the other way so that they would not see their father's nakedness. When Noah awoke from his wine and found out what his youngest son had done to him, he said: Cursed be

Canaan!  The lowest of slaves will he be to his brothers [Gen. 9:20-25].

These verses of Scripture have been misinterpreted to justify the racial oppression of the Black race in everything from slavery in America to apartheid in South Africa.  The fact is that it was Canaan, not Ham his father that was cursed.  Also, it was Noah and not God who did the cursing!  In his embarrassment at being seen naked and in a drunken stupor, he lashed out with a curse.  Understanding what we do about human nature, such a response would not be uncommon even today.  What a terrible perversion of scripture it has been for these many centuries, for such a minor Biblical incident to be used to cause such major pain, dehumanization, and cruelty towards an entire race of people who happen to have been born with dark skin.

# CHAPTER 3

# THANK GOD FOR EGYPT

## EGYPT IN HISTORICAL CONTEXT

There has been a long-standing misunderstanding of the history and cultures of the peoples of Africa. Many have characterized the African continent as a huge area of land, mostly comprised of jungle, and inhabited by savages and fierce beasts. Africa was not thought of as an area where great civilizations might have existed or where great kings could have ruled over vast empires. Although the cultural achievements of Egypt were acknowledged, Egypt was conceived of as a European rather than African territory.

If one but looks at a map of the world, it is obvious that Egypt is in fact a very evident part of Africa. The Sahara Desert, however, does provide a convenient division of the continent, which has come to be perceived as having those nations north of the Sahara being inhabited by European-like people of high culture and noble history. The perception is that those people south of the Sahara area who were dark-skinned people had no culture, and had accomplished nothing worthy of being called history until the European colonialists arrived. The truth is that the history of Africa was already old when Europe was first born.

The distorter's of African history have somehow chosen to ignore the fact that the people of the ancient land, which would later be called Egypt, never called their country by that name. It was called Ta-Merry and sometimes Kemet or Sais. The ancient Hebrews in the Bible called it Mizriam, named after one of the sons of Ham. (Gen. 10:6, 13) Both the Greeks and the Romans referred to the land as "The Pearl of the Nile."

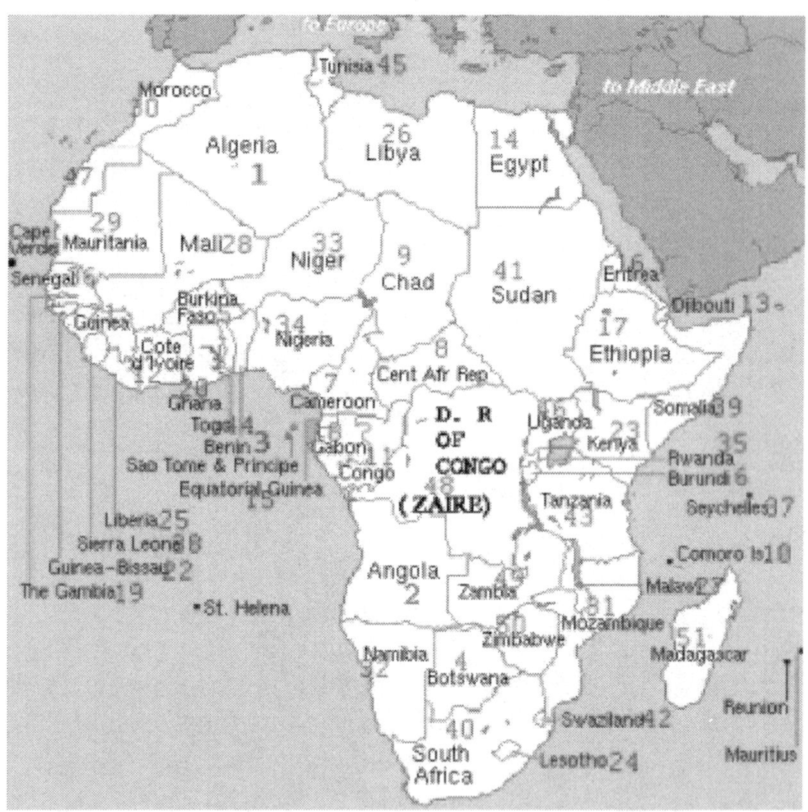


Figure 3

The Greeks gave it the simple name *Aegyptcus*, thus, the name *Egypt* is of Greek origin.[13] The ancient Egyptians were distinctly African people. The great Nile River, that is over four thousand miles long, starts in the South, in the very heart of Africa, and flows to the North. It is considered the world's first cultural highway. Thus, ancient Egypt was composed of many African cultures that traveled north. A nation's history will surely be distorted if only recorded by its enemies and conquerors, but the Egyptians left the best

---

[13] John Henrik Clarke, " African People in World History" ( 1993)

24

history of their own culture.

It was not until the end of the eighteenth century, when a few European scholars learned to decipher Egyptian writing, that this became clear. For example, the highly respected "Papyrus of Hunefer," in the Egyptians written history, *Book of the Coming Forth by Day and Night*, documented the Southern African origins of the ancient Egyptians. "We came from the beginning of the Nile where God Hapi dwells, near the foothills of the mountain of the moon. Kilimanjaro between Kenya and Tanzania, or Rwenzori in Uganda." In Somalia and present-day Zimbabwe, there are ruins of buildings constructed with dress stone and showing a close resemblance to the architecture of early Egypt. The Nile River played a major role in the relationship of Egypt to the nations in Southeast Africa.[14] In many ways, Egypt is the key to ancient African history, and unless Egypt is seen as an African nation, African history becomes distorted.

The invasions of Egypt that started in 1675 BC and continued until after the Roman period brought into Egypt large numbers of people who were not indigenous to the country. The bulk of the Arab population in present-day Egypt has no direct relationship to ancient Egyptian history. Most of them came into Africa in the seventh and eighth centuries during the rapid spread of Islam.[15] The face of Egypt and North Africa was thereafter changed forever.

## EGYPT IN BIBLICAL SIGNIFICANCE

The Bible refers to Egypt over 700 times. As mentioned previously, it was Mizriam, the second son of Ham, one of Noah's three sons, who settled in the area we call Egypt. Apparently during the desertion of Babel (Genesis 11) Mizraim followed his two brothers Cush and Phut to Africa.

---

[14] Ibid, p.24.
[15] John Henrik Clarke, "African People in World History" (1993) P.23.

Cush, called the father of Cushi, meaning Ethiopia, established an empire that extended into China, India and Afghanistan. Phut, according to the great Jewish historian Flavius Josephus, was the founder of Libya, and he called the inhabitants of this new territory Phutites after himself. Mizraim's Egyptians, like the Ethiopians, were masters of architecture, astronomy, medicine, science, art, agriculture, and military technique.[16]

At the height of its power, about 1560 B.C., the Egyptian empire had spread beyond the Nile Valley to Palestine and Syria. The nations that acknowledged Egypt's supremacy routinely sent quantities of ivory, gold, and spices to its temples and courts. In 1240 B.C., following the reign of the last great Pharoah, Ramses II, who is thought to be the Pharoah who oppressed the Israelites, Egypt began to slowly decline.[17] At its height, it was one of the most powerful nations in history.

## ABRAHAM SAVED IN EGYPT

The salvation history of the world is deeply entwined with the African nation of Egypt. In the Book of Genesis chapter 12, we are introduced for the first time to a man who would indeed change the world. His name is Abraham. The three great monotheistic religions of the world, Judaism, Christianity, and Islam all trace their heritage back to this one man, Abraham.

Originally known as Abram "exalted father", Abraham was probably born some 4,000 years ago in the famous Babylonian city known as Ur of the Chaldeans, which was situated in what is now Iraq. He was apparently a wealthy man, the head of a semi-nomadic clan that lived by herding large flocks and by seasonal farming. Perhaps because of an invasion by the Amorites, Abraham's father Terah decided to

---

[16] Julian Ramsses Johnson," The Garden of Eden" ( Nashville: James C. Winston Publishing Com. 1994)

[17] Joyce Andrews, " Bible Legacy of the Black Race" (Nashville: Winston-Derek Publishers, 1993)

move his family to Haran, a prosperous town 500 miles away from Ur in what is now Southeastern Turkey.

It is here that we witness a turning point in Biblical history as God selects this man Abram and his family to be the recipients of His special revelation, care, and promises. At the age of 75, God calls Abraham to leave his country, his people, and even his father's house and go to a land that God has promised him, the alien region of Canaan, some 400 miles to the south. "I will bless them that bless you, and curse them who curse you," said the Lord; "and by you all the families of the earth will be blessed." [Gen. 12:3]

We then get an insight as to why God chose this man above all the men of his generation to develop this special relationship that would touch the world; "So Abraham left, as the Lord had told Him." [Gen.12:4] Abraham was a man of incredible obedience and unshakable faith, the two rare qualities that God required.

We read: "Now there was a famine in the land, and Abraham went down to Egypt to live there for a while because the famine was severe." [Gen. 12:10] Apparently, the land of Egypt still had food and rain while the land in which Abraham was dwelling did not. Here is the first of several instances when Egypt provides refuge and deliverance for Abraham and, therefore, his descendants, which will include he who is called the Savior of the world, Jesus the Christ!

In chapter 15 of Genesis we read: "on that day the Lord made a covenant with Abraham and said, to your descendants I give this land, from the river of Egypt to the great river, Euphrates..." [Gen. 15:17] The Hebrew Bible uses the word *covenant* to describe a binding relationship based on commitment that develops a relationship involving promises and obligations and having the quality of constancy and durability.

A covenant was often sealed in blood and could be terminated only by death. In the covenant God made with Abraham, it would continue to be valid for his descendants forever. The term FRIEND was used exclusively to refer to one's covenant partner. In the entire Bible, Abraham is the only man ever referred to as the *"friend of God."* (James 2:23)

## ABRAHAM'S LINEAGE PRESERVED BY EGYPT

In the Book of Genesis chapters 37-50, we read the story of Joseph and his brothers. Abraham's grandson Jacob, who is also called Israel, had four wives and 11 sons. He showed an over abundance of blatant favoritism to his youngest son Joseph and, as one might assume, it caused terrible rivalry and ultimately hatred between the sons. The conclusion of this conflict is found in chapter 37, where the brothers sell Joseph into slavery to a band of Ishmaelites (Gen. 37:28), who took him down to Egypt where he was sold to an Egyptian by the name of Potiphar, the captain of Pharoah's guard. (Gen. 39:1) Joseph was destined to endure an incredible life that included promotions and unfair devastations. We could outline his life as the following:

I.   PIT (Genesis 37)

II.  POTIPHARS (Genesis 39)

III. PRISON (Genesis 40)

IV.  PRIME MINISTER (Genesis 41-50)

Throughout the story of Joseph we read these recurring words: "now the Lord was with Joseph." (Gen.39:2,21) Somehow, in what would appear to be a saga of tragedy, and mistreatment, we read of a sovereign plan unfolding. It wasn't until many years later when famine had ravaged the land of Canaan and only Egypt had a storehouse of abundant provision that the mystery becomes clear.

God had led Joseph to prepare Egypt for the famine, and they not only had enough to save themselves but also to sell to surrounding neighbors at great profit. When Joseph's own brothers come and bow before him to seek to purchase food to save their family, he finally reveals himself to them and also reveals his revelation concerning God's providential plan:

> Then Joseph said to his brothers, Come close to me. When they had done so, he said, I am Joseph, the one you sold into Egypt!  And now do not be distressed and do not be angry with yourselves for selling me here, because it was to save lives that God sent me ahead of you.  For two years now there has been famine in the land, and for the next five years there will not be plowing and reaping.  But God sent me ahead of you to preserve you for a remnant in the earth and to save your lives with a great deliverance. So, then, it was not you who sent me here, but God. (Gen. 45:4-8)

For the second time we see that God chose the African nation of Egypt to be the land of salvation and preservation for the covenant family of Abraham.  The Genesis account concludes by saying:

> All those who went to Egypt with Jacob, those who were his direct descendants, not counting his son's wives, numbered sixty six persons.  With the two sons who had been born to Joseph in Egypt, the members of Jacob's family, which went to Egypt, were seventy in all. (Gen. 46:26-27)

The descendants of Joseph would stay in Egypt for over four hundred years, would be enslaved and finally delivered by the mighty man called Moses.  When they left this ancient nation they would leave with great riches and a destiny to prepare the world for the coming Messiah.

# THE CHRIST CHILD PROTECTED IN EGYPT

Possibly one of the most overlooked and yet essential texts concerning Egypt's role in the salvation story of the Bible is found in the Gospel of Matthew as follows:

When the Wise Men  had gone, an angel of the Lord appeared to Joseph in a dream as follows: Get up, he said, take the child and his mother and escape to Egypt.  Stay there until I tell you, for Herod  is going to search for the child and kill him.  So he got up, took the child and his mother during the night and left for Egypt, where he stayed until the death of Herod. And so was fulfilled what the Lord had said through the prophet: Out of Egypt I called my son. (Hosea 11:1) When Herod realized that he had been outwitted by the Magi, he was furious, and he gave orders to kill all boys in Bethlehem and its vicinity who were two years old and under, in accordance with the time he learned from the Magi. (Mt. 2:13-16)

Had Herod succeeded in his plot to kill this new born "King of the Jews," Jesus would never have reached maturity, never taught His eternal message of brotherhood, forgiveness and eternal love, and most significantly, never died on the cross and shed His blood to atone for the sins of the entire world. (John 3:16)  The salvation story of the Bible that reaches out to the entire world could not have been fulfilled without the contribution of Africa.

# CHAPTER 4

# OLD TESTAMENT AFRICAN HEROS

It would be futile and insulting to seek to depict the ancient African peoples of Biblical times as paragons of virtue and perfection.  People of all races and heritage all trace their lineage back to the first man Adam, and have inherited his inclination towards sin.  We do read in Genesis 10 about the various descendants of Noah's second son Ham.  The name Ham means "hot" or "heat" and probably refers to "burnt" or "dark skin color."  As mentioned earlier, for Noah and his wife to have produced children of various skin pigmentation's, one or both of them would have had to genetically been black.

The sons of Ham: Cush, Mizriam, Put and Canaan.  The sons of Cush: Seba, Havilah, Sabtah, Raamah, and Sabtecah.  The sons of Raamah:  Sheba and Dedan.
Cush was the father of Nimrod, who grew up to be a mighty warrior on the earth.  He was a mighty hunter before the Lord; that is why it is said, "like Nimrod, a mighty hunter before the Lord."  The first centers of his kingdom were Babylon, Erech, Akkad, and Calneh, in Shinar.  From the land he went to Assyria, where he built Nineveh, Rehoboth Ir, Calah and Resen, which is between Nineveh and Calah; that is the great city.
Mizriam was father of the Ludites, Anamites, Lehabites, Naphthhites, Pathrusites, Casluhites, (from whom the Philistines came) and Caphtorites.
Canaan was the father of Sidon his firstborn, and of the Hittiies, Jebusites, Amorites, Girgashites, Hivites, Arkites, Sinites, Arvadites, Zemarites, and Hamathites.
Later, the Canaanite clans scattered and the borders of Canaan reached from Sidon toward Gerar as far as

Gaza, and then toward Sodom, Gomorrah, Admah and Zeboiim, as far as Lasha. These are the descendants of Ham by their clans and languages, in their territories and nations (Gen. 10: 6-20).

Out of these various clans that descended from Ham, the son of Noah and the alleged founder of the Black race, the Bible tells us of a number of heroes who emerged and who are recorded in the Old Testament. They were men of distinction, courage and honor. We will consider just a few below.

## OLD TESTAMENT AFRICAN HEROS

| | |
|---|---|
| The Cushite Warriors | II Chronicles 21:16 |
| Uriah the Hittite | II Samuel 11:1-21 |
| The Queen of Sheba | I Kings 10:1-13 |
| Ebed Melech | Jeremiah 38:1-10 |
| Zephania | Zephaniah 1:1 |

**Figure 4**

## A NATION OF WARRIORS WHO REFUSED DEFEAT

Cush was the firstborn son of Ham. He moved his family south into the land we know as Africa. He settled in Northeast Africa, near his brother Mizriam (Egypt). Cush is called the father of Cushi, meaning Ethiopia. There are two types of Ethiopians mentioned in Scripture, who differed physically only in hair texture.

The northern Ethiopians had woolly hair while those dwelling in the south had straight hair. There is no genetic reason for the difference in their hair within that period, however, it can be assumed geographically that those who settled closer to the equator obtained hair differentiation due to the heat of the sun.  The Bible also speaks of the Arabian Ethiopians, who were Cushs' offspring living in Midian. (II Chron. 21:16; Hab. 3:7)

The ancient Ethiopians fought continuous wars with the Egyptians, Persians, Hebrews, Assyrians, Arabians and Greeks.  The military conqueror Alexander the Great felt Cush's might in 332 BC. After conquering Egypt easily, the Greeks decided to devastate the Ethiopians. During that adventure, Alexander suffered grief and aggravation, as Cush forced Alexander's once unconquerable army to retreat to Egypt.

Even Rome, in all her glory, was incapable of conquering the mighty Cush. Cush defeated Augustus Caesar around 25 B.C.  He, like Alexander, realized Ethiopians military proficiency, withdrew his forces and made no other effort to venture south of Egypt's border.  Thus, Rome's empire was contained at the northern border of Ethiopia.[18]

## URIAH: A MAN OF UNCOMPROMISING HONOR

In II Samuel chapter 11 we are introduced to a man of African heritage who is one of the most honorable men in the Bible.  His name is Uriah. He was a descendant of Heth, who was the second son of Canaan (Gen. 10:15) son of Ham This was probably the reason Uriah was referred to as the Hittite. The Egyptian and Assyrian monuments described the Negro Hittites as a great race of the North, whose shrewd army was feared for its valor and size.[19]

The Black Hittities were often written about in Scripture for their conflicts with Joshua, David, and Solomon. None of these individuals conquer them.  They remained a powerful nation during the Jewish captivity into Babylon and

---

[18]  John L. Johnson, " The Black Biblical Heritage" ( Nashville: James C. Winston Publishing 1994)

[19]  Ibid p.68

for an additional two centuries thereafter.  Apparently this man Uriah was a convert to belief and faith in Jehovah, the God of the Hebrews.

Uriah was acknowledged to be a loyal and courageous warrior in King David's army.  In fact, we read, in II Samuel 23:39 that he was one of "the thirty" who were called David's "Mighty Men," his elite force which was led by his captain Joab.  The context is found in verse 1.  In II Samuel chapter 11 the story reveals that Uriah is out with King David's army fighting against the Ammonites.  This statement is as follows:

> In the spring, at the time when kings go off to war, David sent Joab out with the king's men and the whole Israelite army. They destroyed the Ammonites and besieged Rabbah.  But David remained in Jerusalem (II Sam.11:1).

It appears that each year after winter had passed the custom was for the king to lead his troops out to battle to secure the border of his kingdom that had been encroached upon by his enemies in previous months.  We do not read that David was ill or that he had other pressing matters of state to contend with.  He simply decided that this year he would not follow the road of his responsibilities, but rather the road of his feelings and stay at home. This decision would not only change David's life and affect the future of his family and his nation; it would also cost an honorable man his very life.

Possibly David felt guilty that his troops were out sleeping in the fields and risking their lives on his behalf, and here he was in the comfort of his palace.  In any case, it appears David had insomnia and could not sleep. (II Sam. 11:2) He went out onto the flat roof of his home to walk and think. From this vantage point, however, he looked down through the open window of a neighbor and saw a beautiful woman bathing.

David sent one of his servants to inquire as to who she was, and it turned out to be the beautiful Black wife of one of his soldiers, Uriah.  Even with this information in hand, the Bible says David sent for her, and "she came to him, and he slept with her...then she went back home." (II Sam. 11:4)  It is tragic to note how fast David's wrong choice, not to be with his troops, led to a wrong action, knowingly committing adultery with the wife of one of his own soldiers! The ramifications of this one night fling became a complicated disaster:

> Then the woman conceived and sent word to David saying, "I am pregnant." (II Sam. 11:5)  David was no doubt unhappy to hear this news but as a veteran leader and problem solver he came up with a quick solution.  He sent a message to Joab and told him to "send me Uriah the Hittite" (II Sam. 11: 6).

Under the guise of wanting a military update on the battle, David debriefs Uriah concerning the success of the army.  He then dismisses Uriah for a night of rest and relaxation with his wife.  His assumption is that surely any soldier who has been away from home for many days will jump at the chance to share some intimate moments with his wife. Perhaps David was projecting on Uriah that which he himself would do if the situation were reversed. According to Scripture the army of Israel was actually not allowed to be sexually intimate during times of war. (I Sam. 21:5)  What David had never considered was the fact that Uriah was in fact a man of honor.

> When David was told, "Uriah did not go home," David, asked him, "Haven't you just come from a long distance, why didn't you go home?"  Uriah said to David, "The ark and Israel and Judah are staying in tents, and my master Joab and my king's men are camped in the open fields.  How could I go to my

house to eat and drink and lie with my wife?  As surely as you live, I will not do such a thing! (II Sam. 10-11).

David was now beginning to worry that his plan was failing and his sin might be revealed.  He prevailed upon Uriah to stay one more night, hoping that his resolve would weaken and he would go home to his wife.  David even went so far as to invite him to his house for dinner and  "David made him drunk," but "in the evening Uriah went to sleep on his mat among the king's servants; he did not go home."

The king was now a desperate man.  Even drunken Uriah had more depth of character than David had sober.  He could not get this African warrior to compromise his values at any price.  So David used Uriah's loyalty against him, and it would cost him his life.  In the morning David wrote a letter to Joab and sent it with Uriah.  In it he wrote, "Put Uriah in the front line where the fighting is fiercest.  Then withdraw from him so he will be struck down and die."  (II Sam. 11:15) Carrying his own death sentence in the King's sealed letter, Uriah reported back to his captain Joab and rejoined his colleagues in defending their nation.  Within twenty-four hours after his return he was placed in an area of great fighting, Joab withdrew the supporting troops, leaving Uriah the Hittite to die. (I Sam 11:18-21)

When Bathsheba heard the news of her husband's death, she went into a period of mourning. However, "after the time of mourning was over, David brought her to his house, and she became his wife and bore him a son.  But the thing David had done displeased the Lord." (I Sam. 11:27) David thought he had pulled off the perfect deception, but God Himself was an eyewitness to the whole tragic event, and He would bring judgment into David's life as a result of his premeditated act of orchestrating the death of a brave and honorable man.

# THE QUEEN OF SHEBA: A WOMAN OF AUTHORITY AND GENEROSITY

The Queen of Sheba, known also as the Queen of the South (Mt. 12:42), was from the Sheba province located in modern Yemen at the southern tip of the Arabian Peninsula, across from Ethiopia. Ancient Arabia was inhabited by two races, the Cushites, (Dedan, Sheba and Raamah, who were offspring of Ham's son Cush, Gen. 10:6) and the Semites, who for ages intermarried, and developed what we recognize as modern day Arabia. The Cushites were the first race to settle the country and were joined by the Semites three centuries later. The name Semite is termed in Arabic lore, "moustaribes," or "foreigners," because of their late arrival.[20]

In I Kings chapter 10, we read of an ancient African Queen who traveled to speak with Solomon, the King of Israel. It is to be noted that Solomon's mother was Bathsheba, former wife of Uriah and a woman of Hamitic heritage. Bathsheba was the daughter of Eliam, son of Ahithophel the Gilonite. (II Sam. 23:34) The Gilonites were Hittite descendants of Canaan who settled the city of Giloh. David the Hebrew King, was Solomon's father, thus making King Solomon a man of mixed Semitic and Hamitic heritage.

When the queen of Sheba heard about the fame of Solomon and his relation to the name of the Lord, she came to test him with hard questions. Arriving at Jerusalem with a very great caravan—with camels carrying spices, large quantities of gold, and precious stone—she came to Solomon and talked with him about all that she had on her mind. Solomon answered all her questions; nothing was too hard for the king to explain to her. When the Queen of Sheba saw all the wisdom of Solomon and the palace he had built, the

---

[20] John L. Johnson, "The Black biblical Heritage" (Nashville: James C. Winston Publishing, 1994)

food on his table, the seating of his officials, the attending servants and cupbearers, and the burnt offerings he made at the temple of the Lord, she was overwhelmed (I Kings 10:1-5).

And she gave the King 120 talents of gold (4 metric tons), large quantities of spices, and precious stones. Never again were so many spices brought in as those the queen of Sheba gave to King Solomon (I Kings 10:10). King Solomon gave the queen of Sheba all she desired and asked for, besides which he had given her out of his royal bounty.  Then she left and returned with her retinue to her own country (v.13).

This ancient African Queen was a woman of wealth, power, and beauty. She was very impressed by the great wisdom of King Solomon and her response to his insights was to give incredibly valuable gifts to the King of the land of Israel.

## EBED MELECH: THE CUSHITE WHO SAVED A PROPHET

Jeremiah was born about 640 B. C. to a priestly family in Anathoth, a village some three miles north of Jerusalem. His father Hilkah was a landowner of some means and was perhaps a descendant of the priest Abiathar, who had been banished to Anathoth by King Solomon for failure to side with him in his struggle for the throne against his older brother Adonijah.[21]

Bible scholars know Jeremiah, as *the weeping prophet.* His heart was broken over the sin and idolatry of the people of Judah, and he had the prophetic foreknowledge from God to know that judgment was coming upon the idolatrous people in the persons of the Babylonians. They would be God's rod of correction for His own covenant people. The

---

[21]  Readers Digest," Great People of the Bible and How They Lived" ( Pleasantville: The Readers Digest Association, Inc. 1994)

king and his officials hated Jeremiah because he told them things they did not want to hear. Even today those who proclaim truth can be incredibly unpopular.

## STUCK IN THE MUD

A story that is sometimes overlooked is one in which the prophet of God was rescued from certain death by the courageous act of an African hero. The story unfolds as follows:

> ...(the King's officials) heard what Jeremiah was telling all the people when he said, "This is what the Lord says: 'Whoever stays in this city will die by the sword, famine or plague, but whoever goes over to the Babylonians will live. He will escape with his life; he will live.' And this is what the Lord says: 'This city will certainly be handed over to the army of the king of Babylon, who will capture it.' Then the officials said to the king, "This man should be put to death. He is discouraging the soldiers who are left in this city, as well as all the people, by the things he is saying to them. This man is not seeking the good of these people but their ruin." "He is in your hands," King Zedekiah answered, "The king can do nothing to oppose you." So they took Jeremiah and put him into the cistern of Malkijah, the king's son, which was in the courtyard of the guard. They lowered Jeremiah by ropes into the cistern: it had no water in it, only mud, and Jeremiah sank down into the mud (Jer. 38:1-6).

It would appear that the prophet's life was near the end. Starvation, dehydration, or suffocation in the mud down in the cistern (well) was to be his frightful end. The cistern would become his tomb, or so it appeared. It is at this crucial moment that a courageous African man steps forward and risks his life to save a life.

# AN ETHIOPIAN HERO

But Ebed-Melech, a Cushite (Ethiopian), an official in the royal palace, heard that they had put Jeremiah into the cistern. While the king was sitting in the Benjamin Gate, Ebed-Melech went out of the palace and said to him, My lord the king, these men have acted wickedly in all they have done to Jeremiah the prophet. They have thrown him into the cistern where he will starve to death when there is no longer any bread in the city. Then the king commanded Ebed-Melech the Cushite, Take thirty men from here with you and lift Jeremiah the prophet out of the cistern before he dies (Jeremiah 38:7-10).

The courage of the African royal official saved the life of the prophet Jeremiah, and allowed him to continue his ministry for Jehovah God. Tragically, the people never did repent or listen to the words of Jeremiah. Many were taken away in captivity to Babylon and others rebelled against Jeremiahs' words to stay in the land, and God would eventually forgive. Instead, they fled to Egypt, taking Jeremiah with them, and thus disappearing from the pages of sacred history.

## ZEPHANIAH: THE CUSHITE WHO WAS A PROPHET

The Bible records that at least one of the prophets whose writings are part of the canon of Scripture was a man of Africa, a Cushite named Zephaniah. Notice his introduction in the Scriptures:

The word of the Lord came to Zephaniah son of Cushi, the son of Gedaliah, the son of Hezekiah, during the reign of Josiah son of Amon, king of Judah  (Zepheniah 1:1).

In this one verse, we learn much about this man.  We learn he is of African descent (son of Cushi), and that he is the great-great grandson of the great King Hezekiah.  He prophesied in the days of Josiah, and he was a contemporary with Jeremiah (see Jeremiah 1:2). Although like Jeremiah, he prophesied of the wrath of God coming on the nation of Judah because of their sin and rebellion. He also looked ahead to a time of blessing and healing. The coming Messianic Kingdom would one day embrace all nations.  He says that for Israel, all afflictions would be over and they would be made, *"a praise among all the people of the earth"* (3:20).

# CHAPTER 5

# THE FAMILY TREE OF JESUS

Everybody has a family lineage or a family tree. It has been said, you cannot choose who your ancestors were, but you can affect your descendants, and that is very true. Every human being is the descendant of a family line dating  back for centuries. We might like to think we all come from royal or heroic stock, but for most of us we have a mixed heritage from people who were a combination of good and bad, righteousness and unrighteousness. So it was also with the family tree of Jesus.

## WAS JESUS A WHITE MESSIAH?

It is one of the tragic misconceptions of history that Jesus of Nazereth had blond hair and blue eyes and was as handsome as any star in a Hollywood movie. The Bible declares just the opposite:

> He had no beauty or majesty to attract us to him, nothing in his appearance that we should desire Him. He was despised and rejected by men, a man of sorrows and familiar with suffering. Like one from whom men hide their faces he was despised, and we esteemed Him not (Isa. 53:2-3).

In the popular sense of present-day American religious culture, Jesus was not a handsome, self-confident, financially prosperous religious leader of his day. He was a simple man with very few material possessions and, at times, had "no place to lay His head." He worked as a carpenter, or more likely a stonemason with his earthly guardian Joseph during his developing years. He had the calluses of a workingman on his hands.

Jesus also could not look to his earthly family heritage to boast of a perfect bloodline. Although he was indeed part of a royal line of many Israelite Kings, his ancestors were as flawed as the rest of humanity. In his family tree, was a famous ruler who had a man killed so he could steal his wife (King David); a man who was sexually intimate with one thousand women and, in his old age, reverted to pagan idolatry (King Solomon); a mad man who sacrificed his own children in fire to the Caananite god Baal, and led his whole country into idolatry (King Manasseh); and a King who became a leper after God judged him for intruding on the office of the priests (King Uzziah).

## Jesus' African Heritage

The New Testament gives us two reports of the lineage of Jesus, one from the Gospel of Matthew and one from the Gospel of Luke. The Bible teaches that in the most literal sense of the word, God was Jesus' Father, as Mary conceived her child as the Holy Spirit came upon her, and not through a natural union of a man and woman. Joseph was in essence Jesus' earthly guardian during his developmental years on earth. Studying the family tree of Jesus, we discover a fascinating truth. There were four Black women in his family lineage.

Matthew 1:1-6 states:

A record of the genealogy of Jesus Christ the son of David, the son of Abraham: Abraham was the father of Isaac, Isaac the father of Jacob, Jacob the father of Judah and his brothers, Judah the father of Perez and Zerah, whose mother was Tamar, Perez the father of Hezron, Hezron the father of Ram, Ram the father of Amminadab, Amminadab the father of Nahshon, Nahshon the father of Salmon, Salmon the father of Boaz, whose mother was Rahab, Boaz the father of

Obed, whose mother was Ruth, Obed the father of Jesse, and Jesse the father of King David. David was the father of Solomon, whose mother was Uriah's wife (Bathsheba)...

Tamar, Rahab, Ruth, and Bathsheba are all women who trace their lineage ultimately to Ham, the traditional father of the Black race. Mary, like thousands of Jews in her day, was of mixed racial heritage. Remember that Moses had an Ethiopian wife (Num. 12:1) and that Joseph married an Egyptian (African) woman and had two sons (Gen. 46:20), Ephriam and Manasseh.

The fact that Mary had a mixed racial heritage and that she was God's special choice to be the earthly mother of His Son, the Messiah of the world, cannot be overemphasized. God chose for the Christ to come into the world via a woman with a multi-cultural lineage that people of all races could identify with Him. According to the North American definition of race in the 17th, 18th, and 19th Century, declaring if one had "one drop of black blood" they were black; Jesus would have been classified as a Colored man!

So what color was Jesus when He walked with His disciples on earth? Probably the same light-brown color of most other Jews who traveled a lot in the hot Mediterranean sun, and had a mixed racial heritage. This is not to say that Jesus and His other Jewish contemporaries were Black Africans; it is merely to say they were clearly not white Europeans either.[22]

## HOW JESUS TURNED WHITE

It is indeed tragic that man is often guided not by historical facts, but rather by his own perceptions. Our perception may be our reality, but that does not necessarily mean that it is true. Sacred history has been badly distorted

---

[22] Keener and Usery, " Black Man's Religion" ( Downers Grove: InterVaristy Press Inc. 1996)

over the years to create the misconception that the heroes of the Bible are all white Europeans and thus the Christian faith is the birth right of the white race. The modern form of racism that projects a belief that people of the lighter hues are somehow superior to people of darker hues was completely unknown in the early centuries of Christianity.

The use of white images as Biblical Christian characters probably started in the 4th Century when Christianity became the official religion of the Roman empire. Most of the portraits, paintings, carvings and sculptures of Biblical figures were produced more than 400 years after biblical times by European artists.[23] The Apostle Paul had indeed been very successful in his missionary work in Europe, and the message continued to spread long after his passing.

From the 14th to the 16th centuries there is a period of Christian art that produced many white images of Biblical characters. The most notable artists of this period were Raphael (1483-1520) and Michelangelo (1475-1564). In 1508, Raphael and Michelangelo were commissioned by Pope Julius II to paint Biblical images. Works produced by Raphael included *Christ Bearing the Cross*, *Madonna*, *Holy Family*, and *The Marriage of Joseph and the Virgin*.

The paintings by Michelangelo on the ceiling of the Sistine Chapel are regarded as a masterpiece of decorative design. This series includes the *History of Moses*, the *Life of Christ*, the *Creation*, the *History of Noah*, the *Prophets* and *the Last Judgment*. He also painted that world famous portrait of the *Last Supper*.

These images were later printed in large illustrated King James Versions of the Bible and passed on by families, from one generation to the next. For many people, these were the earliest images to which they were introduced.[24]

---

[23] James C, Anyike, " Historical Christianity African Centered" (Chicago: Popular Truth Inc. Publishers 1994)

24 James C. Anyike, " Historical Christianity African Centered" ( Chicago: Popular Pub. 1994)

However, there is one very significant problem. Both Raphael and Michelangelo were Italian, and the conclusion of viewers is obvious. Jesus, as well as all of the heroes of sacred history, are white!

This distortion of the facts has been used in recent world history to promote a white Jesus as the leader of a white religion called Christianity. This misinformation has led to the most tragic of consequences. Millions of people have had a distorted sense of their own importance, and millions of others have been made to feel inferior, or at best, second-class citizens in the Kingdom of God. Perhaps somewhere in hell you can hear Satan laughing at the results of this counterfeit reality, and the pain it has caused for centuries.

Mary, the mother of Jesus, would be considered an Afro-Asiatic woman who probably had the complexion of a typical Yemenite, Trinidadian or light-skinned African American woman of today. As we mentioned in a previous chapter, Mathew 2:15 and Hosea 11:1 tell us "Out of Egypt I have called my son." The passage is part of the story of Joseph fleeing to Egypt to hide Mary and baby Jesus from the death threats of King Herod. Can you imagine the divine family as Europeans trying to fit in and hide out in the African nation of Egypt! This is quite doubtful.[25]

Literally, hundreds of shrines of the black Madonna have existed in many parts of North Africa, Europe, and Russia. These icons predate the era of the Renaissance artists who, as we have said, portrayed Jesus as a white European.

## THE CONFUSION TODAY OVER JEWISH HERITAGE

A major contributing factor to the confusion regarding the race of the ancient and first century Israelite is the fact that modern Jews of today are largely white. It is logical to conclude that if the majority of those people who

---

25  Cain Hope Felder, " The Original African Heritage Study Bible"
    (Nashville: Winston-Derek Pub. 1992)

are called Jews are white, their ancestors were white. If these white Jews are the descendants of the ancient Israelites, then the ancient Israelites were white. However, the ancient Israelites were not purely white.

One plausible explanation that is offered is that the majority of modern Jews are actual Jews, though they are not Semitic descendants of the ancient Israelites. The two main types of modern Jews are Ashkenazi and Sephardim. More than 90 per cent of those who identify themselves as Jews are Ashkenazi Jews. Less than 6 percent are Sephardim Jews. The word "Sephardim" comes from the Hebrew word "Sepharad," which means Spain, and is used to identify the Jews who descended from ancestors that lived in Spain until the 15th century.[26]

The actual meaning of Ashkenazi is unclear. The Hebrew word Ashkenaz was used to refer to Germany. The Bible identifies Ashkenaz as the name for a grandson of Japheth. Ashkenazi is used in general to identify those Jews who descended from ancestors who lived in Eastern Europe. It is widely believed that Ashkenazi Jewry originated with a Turkish people called the Khazars. The Khazar Empire accepted Judaism as the state religion, much the same as Rome chose Christianity in the 4th Century.

In 740 A.D. the Khazars chose Judaism for the sake of neutrality. The choice of Judaism allowed them to maintain their sovereignty without choosing Christianity or Islam as their official religion. Either religion would have made them subject to an established religious hierarchy. Judaism had no religious or political hierarchy, but was the foundation from which the other two religions came.[27]

For more than 600 years after their conversion, the Khazars observed Judaism as their official religion. The decline of the Khazar Empire began in 965 A.D. when the Russians

---

[26] James C. Anyike " Historical Christianity African Centered" (Chicago: Popular Truth Inc. Pub. 1994)
[27] Ibid. p. 78

defeated them. They were allowed to remain independent, and continue to practice their Jewish beliefs into the 13th century. The disappearance of the Khazars from their original homeland (north of the Black Sea, Caucasoid Mountains and Caspian Sea) happened at the same time that Jewish immigrants settled in Germany and Poland.

The vast majority of those who identify themselves as Jews today descended from these Eastern European, or Ashkenazi, Jews. They are indeed Jews, but they are not Hebrews or Israelites by descent.[28] Joseph V. Malcioln, author of *How the Hebrews Became Jews,* provides the following categories for modern Jewry:

---

## JEWISH PEOPLE TODAY

**Ashkenazim** - Descendants and mixtures of Hebrews and even Gentiles. Others are proselytes converted several centuries ago.

**Sephardin** - Hebrews of North Africa, Syria, Spain, Portugal, Egypt, Turkey, Arabia, the West Indies and Latin America.

**Falashim** - Hebrews of North, East, and West Africa, particularly Ethiopia.

---

### Figure 5

The Falashim Jews are the most obvious descendants of the Israelites. These Black people claim direct descent from the ancient Israelites and possess ancient Hebrew documents, a claim that cannot be made by Ashkenazi Jews. For more than 2,000 years, there have been rumors that the Ark of the Covenant is in Ethiopia. It is believed by many that the Ark is kept in a temple in the city of Axum and is guarded by a secretive order of monks. Perhaps we will never know, nor do we need to.

---

[28] Ibid p. 83

The point is that the ancestry of Jesus reveals him to be a man with the blood of several races, including African, flowing through His veins.  No race or ethnic group can claim exclusive rights to the Messiah and His work of Grace in this world.  The Apostle John put it the following way:

> For God so loved the world that He gave His only begotten Son, that whosoever believeth in Him shall not perish, but have everlasting life.  For God sent not His Son into the world to condemn the world, but that the world through Him might be saved  (John 3:16-17).

The Messiah Jesus came into the world to provide salvation from the penalty of sin.  He took the place of sinful man on the awful cross to pay the price that man deserved for living in rebellion against a holy God, death.  Jesus did not die for the European descendants of this world, nor for the Asians nor those whose roots take them to the continent of Africa.  He came to die for the debt of all ethnic groups and races. His love is all encompassing.

# CHAPTER 6

# BLACK MINISTERS IN THE NEW TESTAMENT

It is most unfortunate that so many in the faith community have such a distorted concept of the contribution of people of African descent in the development of the New Testament narrative. Many of the key figures of the New Testament church were people of African descent. The concept of racial separation based on skin color was apparently unknown in the first century world. It was certainly unknown in the first century church.

<table>
<tr><td colspan="2" align="center"><u>KEY FIGURES</u></td></tr>
<tr><td>Simon of Cyrene</td><td>Matthew 27:27-32</td></tr>
<tr><td>Simeon called Niger</td><td>Acts 11:1</td></tr>
<tr><td>Lucius of Cyrene</td><td>Acts 11:1</td></tr>
<tr><td>Ethiopian eunuch</td><td>Acts 8:26-35</td></tr>
</table>

Figure 6

## THE MAN WHO CARRIED JESUS' CROSS: UNEVENTFUL BEGINNINGS AND UNBELIEVABLE ENDINGS

The day began with excitement and anticipation for Simon. He had traveled many days from his home in Cyrene, a province of Libya in North Africa. He had come to the Holy City of Jerusalem to attend the feast of Passover. History records that a hundred thousand Jews from Palestine had been settled in the province of Cyrene by Ptolemy Soter

(B. C. 323-285), and the Jewish faith had been embraced by many of the local Gentile population. Simon expected this to be a day of joy and celebration as he along with thousands of others who embraced the Jewish faith would look back to the day centuries before when God had delivered the Hebrews, led by Moses, out of Egypt after 400 years of slavery. What a wonderful day this was likely to be.

Life can change dramatically without any warning. Noah had no idea that God would speak to him that day, and call him to build an ark to deliver his family from the impending flood that would destroy life on earth, and through him the human race would survive (Genesis 6). Abraham had no reason to anticipate at breakfast that morning that before the sun set in the west God would command him to leave his family and his homeland and go to a place that God would show him, and that through him "all nations of the earth would be blessed" (Genesis 12). How could he possibly know that over the centuries the three great monotheistic religions of the world, Islam, Judaism, and Christianity, would all look to him as their patriarch? Young David had been out watching his fathers' sheep and when he came home Samuel the priest anointed him to be King (I Samuel 16). You never know what a day might bring forth.

Surely Simon of Cyrene had no earthly idea that on this day he would touch heaven. As Simon made his way to the Temple he encountered an angry mob. Apparently a trial had just ended and a terrifying drama began to unfold before his eyes, and before he could react or escape, he became a part of the horrible plot.

> Then the soldiers of the governor took Jesus into the common hall, and gathered unto him the whole band of soldiers. And they stripped him, and put on him a scarlet robe. And when they had platted a crown of thorns, they put it upon his head, and a reed in his right hand: and they bowed the knee before him, and mocked him, saying, Hail, King of the Jews! And they

spit upon him, and took the reed and smote him on the head.  And after they had mocked him, they took the robe off from him, and put his own raiment on him and led him away to crucify him.  And as they came out, they found a man of Cyrene, Simon by name: him they compelled to bear his cross (Mt. 27: 27-32).

Simon had come to Jerusalem for a celebration, and now he was humiliated by being forced to participate in a crucifixion, carrying the cross of an unknown criminal! Roman soldiers had the authority to draft citizens for any task (Matthew 5:41).  This was the most gruesome task of all. Crucifixion was the most shameful and painful way to execute a criminal.  Roman citizens ordinarily were not crucified.

Crucifixion in fact, was never mentioned in polite society, so degrading was this form of capital punishment.  It was required that the prisoner carries his own cross (or at least the cross beam), and that he wear a placard around his neck announcing his crime.  That placard was then hung over his head on the cross for all to see. Jesus started off carrying his own cross.  When we remember that He had been awake all night, scourged, and abused by the soldiers, we can conclude that He was exhausted.

Of all the bystanders that day standing in the crowd as Jesus and the soldiers passed by, making their way to Golgotha, the place of execution near the Jerusalem garbage dump, it was Simon, a man from Africa, who was chosen to carry the cross of Jesus.  How could Simon have possibly known when he lifted the blood spattered cross upon his shoulders, that this was the atoning blood of the "Lamb of God," who would take away the sin of the entire world?

At what point on the torturous journey through the streets of the city and up the hill to Mount Calvary did Simon finally understand that when he looked into the eyes of this battered man, he was looking into the very face of God incarnate?

## A GODLY INHERITANCE PASSED ON

The Bible never tells us exactly when it happened, but by the end of that fateful day, Simon of Cyrene became a believer in Jesus as the Christ.  It was a belief that would transform his life and a message he would carry home to his wife and children.  How do I know this is true? Mark's description of the day of crucifixion and the drafting of Simon to carry Jesus' cross, refers to him as, "the father of Alexander and Rufus." (Mark 15:21)   Mark's Gospel was written primarily to the Roman readers and the readers apparently knew these young men.  The Apostle Paul, writing nearly 20 years later to the church at Rome declared his personal friendship with this family by stating, "Greet Rufus, chosen in the Lord, and his mother and mine" (Romans 16:13).

## THE MEN WHO ESTABLISHED A MULTI-RACIAL CHURCH

### Africans Present on the Birthday of the Church

In the Book of Acts, chapter 2, we read of the outpouring of the Holy Spirit upon the believers who had gathered in an upper room in Jerusalem.  Jesus Himself had told them not to depart from Jerusalem, "but wait for the promise of the Father, which, he saith, ye have heard of me. For John truly baptized with water; but ye shall be baptized with the Holy Ghost not many days hence" ( Acts 1: 4-5).

So it was on the day of the Jewish Feast of Pentecost, an annual celebration fifty days after the harvest, that Jews from throughout the Roman Empire and other parts of the world made a pilgrimage to Jerusalem to give thanks to God for the harvest he had provided.  With the stage set and all the players in place, God himself stepped in to unfold a drama that is still being played out to this very day.  The story is as follows:

> And when the day of Pentecost was fully come, they were all with one accord in one place.  And suddenly there came a sound from heaven like a rushing mighty wind, and it filled all the house where they were sitting.  And there appeared unto them cloven tongues like as of fire, and it sat upon each of them.  And they were filled with the Holy Ghost, and began to speak with other tongues as the Spirit gave them utterance. And there were dwelling at Jerusalem Jews, devout men, out of every nation under heaven.  Now when this was noised abroad, the multitude came together, and were confounded, because that every man heard them speak in his own language.  And they were all amazed and marveled, saying one to another, behold, are not all these which speak Galileans?  And how hear we every man in our own tongue, wherein we were born? Parthians and Medes, and Elamites, and dwellers in Mesopotamia, and in Judea and Cappodocia, in Pontus and Asia, Phyrigia and Pamphylia, in Egypt, and in the parts of Libya about Cyrene, and strangers of Rome, Jews and Proselytes, Cretes and Arabians, we do hear them speak in our tongues the wonderful works of God (Acts 2:1-11).

The key point to focus on when viewing the roll call on the Day of Pentecost is the multi-cultural constituency that had gathered.  People of European descent are mentioned, and people of Arabian ancestry were clearly represented. There were of course Jews of Hebrew lineage at the religious celebration, but there were also people from Africa in attendance, with Egypt and Libya mentioned by name.  These would have been proselyte Jews who had embraced the Jewish religious faith even though not of Hebrew lineage.

Because the congregation on the Day of Pentecost was both interracial and multi-cultural, so was the first century church as the story goes on to declare that "about three thousand" became believers in Jesus as the Christ that day (Acts 2: 41) and afterwards returned to their various homes around the Roman Empire declaring their new found faith in Jesus as Messiah.

## WE WANT TO BE A NEW TESTAMENT CHURCH

It is a popular cry by pastors and congregations today to declare they want to be nothing less than a New Testament church following New Testament teachings, and expecting New Testament signs and wonders.  My response to such noble declarations is simply to ask, "which New Testament church do you wish to be?"  The Corinthian church was indeed a church where spiritual gifts seemed to be mightily demonstrated, but there were highly volatile divisions (I Cor. 1:10-17), a terrible battle with immorality (I Cor. 5:1-2), and an embarrassing lack of hospitality and good manners (I Cor.11:17-21).

What about the Galatian church, who the apostle Paul rebuked for turning from the gospel of the grace of God to follow another gospel that required works to be saved? (Gal. 1:6-7) Or, would you like to be the church of Ephesus, whom Jesus himself condemned for leaving their first love? (Rev. 2:4). Then there is the very first church, which was established after Pentecost in Jerusalem whose pastor was James, the Lord's brother (Acts 15:13).  This church was exclusively Jewish in composition and had a real struggle over the issue of Gentiles coming into the faith of Christ as a universal savior.

Many could not tolerate the concept that in the church of Jesus Christ no racial or ethnic group is superior; all are one in Him.  At the very least these Jewish believers felt that the Gentiles must begin to follow the Law of Moses as they did, to truly be saved (Acts 15:1). Fortunately wisdom prevailed and the decision of the council at Jerusalem was not to make it difficult for the Gentiles who were turning to God by adding an unneeded burden to their newfound faith (Acts 15:19).

## A MULTI RACIAL MODEL

Persecution ultimately scattered the church from Jerusalem after the martyrdom of Steven (Acts 7:54-60). Some people fled to Antioch and began to proclaim the Gospel of Christ to these people (Acts 11:19-21) and a large number of converts were made. When word got back to the mother church in Jerusalem that even the gentiles were turning to Jesus as the Messiah they sent the apostle Paul and Barnabas, the wise and godly leaders, to Antioch where they remained for a full year (Acts 11:22-24). We are also told that the disciples were first called Christians at Antioch (Acts 11:25).

It is the Antioch church that has left us a wonderful legacy of racial diversity and spiritual vitality. The Bible records in Acts 11:1 that, "in the church at Antioch there were prophets and teachers: Barnabas, Simeon called Niger, Lucius of Cyrene, Manaen (who had been brought up with Herod the tetrarch) and Saul." Two of the five primary leaders in this New Testament congregation were men from Africa. Simeon was apparently known by both his Hebrew name and by his Latin name, Niger, meaning "dark" or "black." This man was clearly a Black man who functioned as either a prophet or a teacher in this prominent church.

The issue of race and color were simply not a factor. Lucius also was an African minister from Cyrene in northern Libya, the same region from which Simon of Cyrene had come. He was the man who carried Jesus' cross.

# THE MAN WHO BROUGHT THE GOSPEL TO AFRICA

The nineteenth century was considered The Great Century for Christian missionary activity.[29] It was during that era that the names of Robert Morrison (China), William Carey (India), Adoniram Judson (Burma), Hudson Taylor (China), and David Livingstone (Africa) became prominent. However, it would be a distortion of the truth to conclude that it was a white European missionary that first brought the message of Christianity to the continent of Africa. The Bible itself tells the story of how the message of God's love first reached the people of this great land.

## A Prophecy Given

Perhaps some seven hundred years before Christ the Psalmist David declared, "Princes shall come out of Egypt; Ethiopia shall soon stretch out her hands to God" (Psalm 68:31). This fulfillment of David's words is presented as follows:

## A Prophecy Fulfilled

Now the angel of the Lord said to Philip, "Go south to the road, the desert road that goes down from Jerusalem to Gaza." So he started out, and on his way he met an Ethiopian eunuch, an important official in charge of all the treasury of Candace, queen of the Ethiopians. This man had gone to Jerusalem to worship, and on his way home was sitting in his chariot reading the book of the prophet Isaiah. The Spirit told Philip, "Go to that chariot and stay near it." Then Philip ran up to the chariot and heard the man reading Isaiah the prophet. "Do you understand what you are reading?" Philip asked. "How can I," he said, "unless someone explains it to me?" So he invited Philip up to

---

[29] J. Herbert Kane, "A Concise History of the Christian World Mission," (Grand Rapids: Baker book House, 1978)

sit with him. The eunuch was reading this passage of Scripture: He was led like a sheep to the slaughter, and like a lamb before the shearer is silent, so he opened not his mouth. In his humiliation he was deprived of justice. Who can speak of his descendants? For his life was taken from the earth. The eunuch asked Philip, Tell me, please, who is the prophet talking about, himself or someone else?" Then Philip began with that very passage of Scripture and told him the good news about Jesus (Acts 8:26-35).

Who was this man from Ethiopia? Apparently he was the finance minister for Candace, queen of the Ethiopians. He was also a proselyte Jew, having embraced the faith of the Hebrews in both their God and their Scriptures. The Jews had two classifications of Gentile converts: "Proselytes of righteousness" for those who had fully adhered to Judaism, and "Proselytes of the gate," for those who either by reason of physical impairment or other reasons could not be given full access to temple worship (Deut. 23:1-4).

This man apparently fulfilled the requirements of the former classification and had traveled over a thousand miles across Africa to reach Jerusalem to worship in the temple there. His conversion experience on his way home and the fact that, "he went on his way rejoicing" (Acts 8:39) gives us the insight that he returned to his homeland as possibly the first Christian evangelist, sharing the good news about God's Son. It would appear from Scripture that Christianity was known in Africa before it was known in Europe. [30]

Today Ethiopia still retains the influence of this government official and his message after nearly two thousand years. The British writer C.F. Rey in his book, <u>Unconquered Abysinnia</u> (Ethiopia), declares that Ethiopia was a great nation when the first book of the Bible was written, and was practicing Christianity while Europe was still worshiping Thor

---

[30] Ibid, p.102

and Odin.

The American writer J.H. Shaw, in his book, <u>Ethiopia,</u> states, that Ethiopia had instituted Christian churches throughout its land long before William the Conqueror set foot in England and a thousand years before Columbus discovered the New World.[31]  What a wonderful truth.  It was a man from Africa who brought the message of eternal salvation to Africa proclaiming the love of Jesus Christ to all who would hear.

---

[31] Paul Johnson, " A History of Christianity" ( New York: Atheeneum Publishers 1977) p.231.

# CHAPTER 7

# EARLY CHURCH FATHERS FROM AFRICA

The Book of Acts is considered to be the history book of the first century church.  Luke, a physician by profession, also became a fine and conscientious historian. Dr. Luke documented the people, places, and various incidents that the first Christians encountered in seeking to both live out and share their faith in Jesus as the Messiah and savior of the world.

After the death of the Apostles, who were eye witnesses of Christ's work, and their converts, the church continued to grow although having to endure many years of persecution and violent opposition within the Roman Empire. It was not until 313 A.D. that Constantine and his co-emperor Licinius published the Edict of Milan, making Christianity legal in the Roman Empire and bringing persecution officially to an end.

Although the New Testament tells about the Apostle Paul's successful evangelism into Europe and the strength and influence of the Palestinian Christian community, it was actually in North Africa where Christianity truly matured.  Of the men that history refers to with respect and appreciation as the early Church Fathers, many of them were not from Europe at all, but rather from North Africa.

One must understand in the context of history that the Roman Empire stretched across Europe and into Northern Africa and Palestine.  We must not minimize the influence of Roman thought and culture on these areas, but we also must acknowledge the fact that it was on African soil that great Christian thinkers and leaders were born and trained, and their impact on the kingdom of God is felt to this very day.

# TERTULLIAN (150-230 A.D.)

History records that a dynamic and distinctive Christian church emerged in Northern Africa in the second century.  Enthusiastic, immensely courageous, utterly defiant of the secular authorities, and much persecuted.[32]  It was from this environment that one of the first African born Christian scholars emerged.  His full name was Quintus Septimius Florens Tertullian, and he is considered the father of Latin theology and church language, and one of the greatest men of Christian antiquity.[33]  His impact is felt to this day.

Tertullian was born in Carthage in 150 A.D. and was educated as a lawyer.  He lived a very immoral life well into his thirties before embracing the Christian faith. His conversion radically changed his life. There is some evidence that Christian Zealots and Essenes who had a very early tradition of militancy and resistance to secular authority evangelized Carthage and other areas of Africa.  Tertullian embodied this tradition.[34]

Around 203 A.D. Tertullian became a Montanist.  The Montanists were a very strict sect of Christians who lived disciplined lives of fasting, prayer, celibacy and regarded martyrdom as a most honorable service.[35]  It was Tertullian who declared, "the blood of the martyrs is the seed of the church."[36]  He was a brilliant thinker who rejected strongly the teachings of a contemporary theologian named Marconi who sought through rationalist argument to reconcile Christian teaching to Greek Philosophy.

---

[32] Paul Johnson, " A History of Christianity" ( New York: Atheneum Publishers, 1977) p.45

[33] Philip Schaff, " Spiritual Leadership" ( Chicago: Moody Press, 1910)

[34] Paul Johnson, "A History of Christianity" (New York: Ttheneum Publishers, 1977) p.48

[35] James C. Anyike, " Historical Christianity African Centered" (Chicago: Popular Truth Inc. Pub. 1994) p.116.

[36] Robert Payne, "The Christian Centuries," (New York: W.W. Norton and Co., 1966) p.90

Tertullian argued; "What has Athens to do with Jerusalem? What has the Academy to do with the Church? What have heretics to do with Christians? Our instruction comes from the porch of Solomon, who had himself taught that the Lord should be sought with simplicity of heart. Away with all attempts to produce a Stoic, Platonic, and dialectic Christianity."[37] He clearly saw it as unacceptable to mix the philosophies of the world with the teachings of Christ.

Tertullian's theological focus seemed to be similar to that of the Apostle Paul, building his belief system on simple faith in the finished work of Christ on the cross coupled with a genuine gratitude to God for his grace and forgiveness extended towards man. He summarized his Christian beliefs with this paradox; "The Son of God was born, I am not ashamed of it because it is shameful; the Son of God died, it is credible for the very reason that it is silly; and having been buried he rose again, it is certain because it is impossible."[38] With this thought provoking insight Tertullian passed on into eternity to meet the Lord he had served so faithfully.


## CYPRIAN (200-258 A.D.)

One of the greatest bishops of the early church was Cyprian, Bishop of Carthage. In 246 A.D., when in his mid forties, Cyprian went through a dramatic conversion experience, finding in Christian baptism a miraculous release from the vices that enchained him. He was a wealthy man, a lawyer, skilled in magical arts.[39] Of his transformation he wrote to his friend Donatus, "I myself was held in bonds by the innumerable errors of my previous life. I was disposed to

---

[37] Paul Johnson, "A Histroy of Christianity," (New York: Atheneum Publishers, 1977) p. 48

[38] James C. Anyike, " Historical Christianity African Centered" ( Chicago: Popular Truth Inc. Pub. 1994) p. 17.

[39] Elizabeth Isichi, " A History of Christianity in Africa" (Grand Rapids, Michigan: William B. Eerdsman Pub. 1995) p.35.

acquiesce in my clinging vices, and because I despaired of better things, I used to indulge my sins as if they were actually parts of me. But after that, by the help of the water of new birth a second birth had restored me to a new man."

He was greatly influenced by the ministry and teaching of Tertullian. Only two years after being baptized he was appointed Bishop and became the head of the whole North African clergy.[40] Cyprian held this position for over ten years. During his reign he had to battle both persecution from outside the church and heresies and controversies from within the church.

Cyprian concluded that the only way to keep the Christian church together was to gather together the developing threads of ecclesiastical order and authority and weave them together into a tight system of absolute control.[41] By establishing a carefully graded hierarchy, beginning with Christ and the Apostles and continued by the work of Bishops and priests, Cyprian believed the Church could be protected from fragmentation and heresy.

He did, however, become involved in a controversy in 256 A.D. over the question of Roman judicial authority over other bishops and clergy, referring to major geographical areas of religious responsibility. From the first to the fourth centuries there were three main centers of Christianity. They were Alexandria in Egypt, Antioch in Syria, and Rome in Italy. Cyprian challenged the power of the Bishop of Rome over the other Bishops.[42]

The persecution of Christians by the Roman Emperor Valerian brought Cyprian's active labors to a close. He was sent into exile for eleven months, then tried before the proconsul, and condemned to be beheaded. When the

---

[40] Philip Schaff, " History of the Christian Church Volume II: Ante-Niene Christianity AD 100-325" Grand Rapids: Eerdmans Pub. Com 1910)

[41] Paul Johnson, "A History of Christianity," (New York: Atheneum Publishers, 1977) p.59

[42] James C. Anyike, "Historical Christianity African Centered," (Chicago: Popular Truth Pub., 1994) p.121

proconsul, and condemned to be beheaded. When the sentence was pronounced, he said: "Thanks be to God," knelt in prayer, tied the bandage over his eyes with his own hand, gave to the executioner a gold coin, and died with the dignity and composure of a hero.[43] The great Bishop of Carthage realized his ultimate dream to die a martyr for Christ.

## ORIGEN (185-254 A.D.)

Without question one of the most brilliant minds of the second and third century was Origen. He was born of Christian parents in Alexandria in Egypt in 185 A.D. His father died a martyrs' death under the persecution of the Roman Emperor Septimus Severus in 202 A.D. Origen was seventeen years old when his father died and at the age of eighteen he was named head of the Catechetical School of Alexandria.[44] This institution was a major contributor to the development of early Christianity in Africa. It was the prototype of the modern theological seminary. From the School of Alexandria came the first systems of Christian theology. It was not only a seat of academic learning and intellectual defense of Christianity, but also a center for the evangelization and missionary enterprise throughout the Eastern Roman Empire.[45]

The greatest contribution of Origen was to create a new science, Biblical theology, whereby every sentence in the scriptures was systematically explored for hidden meanings. In his book, <u>First Principles,</u> he developed a Christian philosophy from which it was possible to interpret every aspect of the

---

[43] Philip Schaff, " History of the Christian Church Volume II: Ante- Nicene Christianty AD 100-325" (Grand Rapids: Eerdmans Pub. Com. 1910) p. 845.
[44] Paul Johnson, " A History of Christianity" New York: Atheneum Publishers 1977)
[45] Aziz S. Atiya, " History of Eastern Christianty" ( South Bend : University of Notre Dame 1968)

world.[46] In this work Origen wrestles with the ultimate beliefs of a Christian, demanding answers to hard questions. What is God? What is the Son? What is the Holy Ghost? What are angels? Why was the universe created?[47] These are the very fundamental questions of the Christian faith that many seek answers to even today. In 249 A.D. Origen was tortured under the persecution of the Emperor Decius. He survived the torture and lived for six more years before dying in 255 AD.[48] A great theologian from North Africa had died, but his theological contributions live on even today.

## AUGUSTINE (354-540 A.D.)

Of all the Church Fathers from the early centuries of Christianity, none is held in higher regard than that of Augustine. He is one of the four great fathers of the Latin Church. He has been called more profound than Ambrose, his spiritual father, more original and systematic than Jerome, his contemporary and correspondent, and intellectually far more distinguished than Gregory the Great, the last of the series.[49] Next to the Apostle Paul, who supplied the basic theology, he did more to shape Christianity than any other human being.[50]

Aurelius Augustine was born on November 13, 354 A.D. at Talsgate, a small village in the fertile province of Numidia in North Africa, and he died on August 28, 430 A.D., living a total of seventy-six years.[51] The town of Talsgate

---

[46] Paul Johnson, "A History of Christianity," (New York: Atheneum Publishers, 1977) p.58

[47] Robert Payne, "The Christian Centuries," (New York: W.W. Norton Co., 1966) p. 86

[48] James C. Anyike " Historical Christianty African Centerd" (Chicago: Popular Truth Inc. Pub. 1994) p.119.

[49] The Encyclopedia Britannica, 9th edition (1878)

[50] John L. Johnson, "The Black biblical Heritage," (Nashville: Winston-Derek Pub., 1994) p. 112

[51] Philip Schaff, " History of the Christian Church Volume II: Ante- Nicene Christianity AD 100-325" (Grand Rapids: Eerdmans Pub. Com. 1910) p.990

was a province of Rome at the time of Augustine, and is now located in the country of Algeria.  His father's name was Patricius, and was apparently a fairly wealthy patrician in the community.  His mother was Monica, who unlike her husband enthusiastically followed the teachings of Christianity.

Augustine's early life was characterized by great intelligence and passionate excess.  He fathered a child out of wedlock and joined the sect called the Manichees. Mani was a Persian who died in 260 A.D. He had attempted to synthesize the various faiths known to him.  The religion he founded lasted a thousand years and won converts from Rome to China, and  left a great literary inheritance in a variety of languages, including Coptic.[52]  The teachings of the Manichees were  characterized  by  intense  pessimism  about  the potentialities of human nature and its inherent goodness. Manichees were passionate, self disciplined, righteous and obstinate.[53]    These various components for some reason attracted the young Augustine.

Augustine was highly regarded within this sect, but the consistent prayers and pleading of his mother Monica, and his exposure to Bishop Ambrose of Milan led to his ultimate conversion.  He left Africa for Rome to become a teacher.  He was a brilliant young law professor who had been invited to teach rhetoric at the University of Milan.  By the time he arrived in Milan to begin this assignment he had begun to have serious doubts about his beliefs in Manichaeism.  On the day of his historic conversion, things began in a most unspectacular way.

He was staying in a villa with his mother and close friend Alyphus when Pontitianus, an officer of the Imperial household, an African and a Christian, came by to call on them.  On the table, which had been marked out for a game

---

[52]  Elizabeth Isichi, " A History of Christianity in Africa" (Grand Rapids, Michigan: William B. Eerdsman Pub. 1995) p.39
[53]  Paul Johnson, " A History of Christianity" New York: Atheneum Pub. 1977)

of dominoes, Pontitianus found a volume of the Epistles of Saint Paul. Augustine had been studying them, but without any deep interest. Pontitianus expressed his surprise at finding the volume and told the story of his own conversion, describing at some length the untroubled delights of the Christian, his sure faith, and his certain knowledge of the path to be followed.[54]

This encounter with a friend from Africa so stirred Augustine that when the man left, his mind was in torment. He burst into a flood of tears and rushed out into the garden, throwing himself on the ground beneath a fig tree. He would later declare, "Thou hast made us for thee, and our heart is restless till it rests in Thee."[55] At this critical moment with tears flowing and conviction of his own sin pounding in his chest Augustine heard a child's voice say, "Tolle, lege," ("take up and read"). He immediately arose and went back into the house to pick up the scriptures again and read in silence the following passage: "Not in rioting and drunkenness, not in chambering and wantonness, not in strife and envying. But put ye on the Lord Jesus Christ, and make no provision for the flesh to fulfill the lusts thereof" (Rom. 8:13,14).

He later wrote in his famous work <u>Confessions of Saint Augustine</u> viii, 30, "I had neither desire nor need to read farther. As I finished the sentence, as though the light of peace had been poured into my heart, all the shadows of doubt dispersed. Thus hast thou converted me to Thee, so as no longer to seek either for wife or other hope the world, standing fast in that rule of faith in which Thou so many years before hadst revealed to my mother."

This incredible conversion experience occurred in the summer of 386 A.D. The visit of an African soldier to the home of the African-born scholar was destined to have an incalculable influence on the development of the Christian

---

[54] Ibid

[55] Philip Schaff, " History of the Christian Church Volume II: Ante- Niene Christianity AD 100-325 1910)

religion around the world. Augustine wrote an enormous amount. Much of what he wrote was influenced by the events of his own day and from his personal experiences, with a great deal of his writings surviving in their original form. For a thousand years he was the most popular of the Church Fathers. The medieval European libraries contained over 500 complete manuscripts of his classic work, <u>City of God</u>. In this book he designed a great apologetic treatise in vindication of Christianity and the Christian Church. A philosophy of history from a Christian worldview was developed, partially to give perspective to the crumbling ruins of the Roman Empire in his day.

The second great work of Augustine is called <u>Confessions</u>, written around 397 A.D. shortly after he became the Bishop of Hippo in North Africa. In this volume he transparently reveals the agonies of his own life of struggle with the temptations of the flesh and the joy and peace he ultimately found in the forgiveness of his sins by Jesus Christ. Throughout his years of ministry and leadership he would deal with a number of theological controversies within the church, as well as dangerous persecutions from without. Augustine lived to see both the moral and military decay of the once mighty Empire of Rome.

In 410 A.D. Rome was invaded by the Goths, led by Alaric, an Arian Christian. The siege produced great hunger in Rome and some people resorted to cannibalism to survive. In 429 A.D. the Vandals invaded North Africa. Like the Goths, the Vandals were Gothic speaking Arians with white skin and blond hair. In their destructive conquest they destroyed churches, basilicas, cemeteries, monasteries, and houses of prayer. Augustine died in 430 A.D. while at his monastery in Hippo. The city remained under siege until 439 A.D.[56] On his death bed, with the Vandals at the gate of the city, Augustine prayed from his room:

---

[56] James C. Anyike, " Historical Christianity African Centered" (Chicago: Popular Truth Inc. pub. 1994) p.125.

I ask God to deliver this city from its enemies, or if that may not be, that He may give us strength to bear His will, or at least that He may take me from this work and receive me into His bosom. As he lay dying he could see this text written above his bed: "Man goeth forth unto his work and to his labor until evening."[57]

The evening had finally come for Augustine and his labor was complete. With sounds of war outside the city he died with peace within his heart.

---

[57] Robert Payne, "The Christian Centuries," (New York: W.W. Norton Co, 1966) p. 142

# CHAPTER 8

# AFRICAN-AMERICAN RELIGIOUS PIONEERS

To appreciate the journey and contribution of people of African descent to the development of Christianity in America it is necessary to look back at a brief time line to give us an overview.  One cannot help but be amazed once again at man's incredible ability to live a life of blatant contradiction and possibly not even realize it.  Humans are indeed capable of compartmentalizing our lives, living with the illusion that what is transpiring in one are of our lives somehow will have no influence on other areas.  In reality this is seldom the case.

That people who enthusiastically and boldly proclaimed the message of Christ and sought to establish a nation based on Biblical principles, could act with such cruelty and insensitivity to fellow human beings who happened to have a darker skin pigmentation for the sake of financial gain, is in retrospect, astounding.  How did such a universal tragedy unfold?

The overview of over 300 years of African history on American soil in just a few pages can cause us to miss the impact of all that transpired.  There is not enough time to review all the pain, or reflect on the entire list of hero's that emerged during that era.  However, it is essential to focus on at least a few of the personalities that so powerfully influenced the development of Christianity in America across several denominations. Some of the people we will mention are listed in the time line of the 18th and 19th Century (see appendix A) while others emerged in the 20th Century, and the impact of their ministry still continues into the new millennium. Following are just a few of the truly outstanding African-

American individuals who have made significant contributions to the growth of Christianity in America.

## TWO MEN WHO REJECTED THE SEPARATE ALTAR

It would have been wonderful had the church community in colonial America modeled racial equality by applying the teachings of scripture that declare that in Christ, "there is neither Jew nor Greek, slave nor free, male nor female, for you are all one in Christ Jesus" (Gal. 3:28). Sadly, that was not the thinking of many early Christians.

In 1786 the membership of Saint George's Methodist Episcopal Church in Philadelphia included both Blacks and Whites. However, the white members met that year and decided that a change should be made and all Black members should sit in the very back of the newly constructed balcony. This area was reserved for slaves and was known as the slave gallery.[58] At the time there was an estimated 10,000 Blacks living in Philadelphia. Six thousand were free and four thousand were still slaves.

Two Black lay preachers, Absalom Jones and Richard Allen, learned of the decision on the following Sunday. During the time of prayer at the altar they were interrupted by one of the ushers and told to move to the balcony. Absalom Jones is reported to have said, "Wait until prayer is over, and I will get up and trouble you no more."[59] After finishing the prayer time Jones, Allen and the entire black constituency walked out, never to return.

---

58  George Bragg, " History of  the Afro- American Group of the Episcopal Church" ( Baltimore: Church Adovacte Press 1922) p. 39
59  Ibid p. 42

# BLACK EPISCOPAL PIONEERS

## THE FIRST BLACK PRIEST IN AMERICA  (18th Century)

### Absalom Jones (1746-1818 A.D.)

If the greatness of a man is to be determined by his accomplishments, courage to overcome adversity and the ability to influence others to follow him, then Absalom Jones surely qualifies for the distinction of being a great man. Absalom was born a slave in Sussex County, Delaware on November 6, 1746. He taught himself to read and his primary source of literature was the Bible. At an early age he had a thorough knowledge of the New Testament. At the age of 16 Absalom's owner took him to Philadelphia where he served as a clerk and handyman in a retail store. He was allowed to work for himself in the evenings and to keep his earnings.

Jones was married in 1766, and through hard work and determination was able to purchase his own and his wife's freedom by the age of 38, and also to purchase his own house. During this time he also met Richard Allen as they joined in ministry in the integrated congregation of St. George's Methodist Episcopal Church. They remained life-long friends, and their ministry had a very positive effect at St. George's causing the church to grow substantially.

The unfortunate conflict over the slave gallery issue caused these two Black leaders to leave St. George's and in 1792, under the leadership of Absalom Jones, The African Church was organized as a direct outgrowth of the Free African Society. The Society embraced the philosophy that the Christian faith was both deeply spiritual and extremely practical. A great deal of time, energy, and resources were used to reach out in benevolence to help widows and orphans, to assist the sick in their pain, and to provide finances for burial expenses to those in the Black community who could not afford them.

At no time was this commitment more obvious than during the late summer of 1793 when yellow fever was first diagnosed near the waterfront in Philadelphia.  In less then 100 days, an estimated 10% of the city population lay dead.  Those who could afford to flee abandoned the city.  Mayor Matthew Clarkson issued a desperate plea for civic-minded volunteers "contribute their aid in the present distress."[60]  The Free African Society, led by Absalom Jones and Richard Allen, bravely answered the call.  Comforting those in terrible pain and suffering, giving hope to families facing loss, and by their courageous example demonstrating their faith in God, the Black community won the respect of many for such a heroic ministry of love.

In 1794, The African Church building was erected with the help of Episcopalians and Quakers.  Both Allen and Jones wished to affiliate with the Methodists, but the majority of the congregation favored the Episcopal Church.  Absalom Jones led the African Church in applying for membership to Bishop William White of Philadelphia, while Richard Allen withdrew with a remnant of the congregation to join with the Methodists.

The African Church soon became St. Thomas African Episcopal Church, and Absalom Jones was ordained a Deacon. Nine years later he was ordained as a Priest, thus becoming the first African-American Priest in American history. Continuing to fulfill his vision of the church, touching the needs of hurting people on earth as we prepare for our time in heaven, he also founded schools for his people, established an insurance company for Blacks, and protested slavery and oppression in every form.  Absalom Jones died on February 13, 1818.

---

[60] Joanne C. Blascoe, " A Narrative of the proceedings of the Black People..."(Missouri: Independence National Historical Park Pub. 1993)

# SCHOLAR, ACTIVIST, and MAN OF GOD (19th Century)

## Alexander Crummel  (1819-1898 A.D.)

Alexander Crummel was born on March 3, 1819 in New York City.  He was educated primarily at the Oneida Institute in Whitesboro, New York.[61]  His father had fled slavery and insisted his son receive the best education at that time available to a Black man. To supplement his training he also worked with private tutors. As an adult he became a scholar, college professor, preacher, missionary, a proponent for the emigration of Blacks to Africa, and an advocate for African-American self-help.  His life is a story of vision and passion for justice and equality.

In 1839 he sought admission to the General Theological Seminary in New York, but was rejected. He was finally ordained in Boston in 1844.  Crummell left the United States for England and then Liberia in West Africa in 1847. He served twenty years on the faculty of Liberia College as a missionary under the Episcopal Church. He returned to the United States in the early 1870's, finding racism among the mulattos of Liberia to finally be intolerable.[62]

In 1873 he moved to Washington D.C. where he was appointed missionary at large to the Black community.  It was in Washington that he planned and realized his vision of the church in the Black community.  Crummell believed the church should be a place of worship and social service.

In 1880 he established St. Luke's Church, which became a beacon of hope for the Black community, and place of learning and mentoring for other Black men with a similar perspective of the role and function of the local church. Crummel took the lead in encouraging black ministers to join together and establish charitable institutions for the benefit of the Black community.  He also organized the Black Episcopal

---

[61] The Encycolpedia Briticanica Vol. 8, p. 263
[62] Randall Burktte, " Black Apostles" ( Boston: G.K. Hall Co. 1978)

clergy to fight racism in the church at large.  In 1897 he was among those who formed the forty-member Negro Academy for the promotion of science, literature and the arts.[63]  There is little doubt that this organization was an inspiration later to civil rights activist and founder of the NAACP, Dr. W.E.B. DuBois' idea of the "talented tenth."

One of Crummell's most bold and courageous acts was accomplished on September 22, 1886 at the Fourth Annual Convocation of Colored Clergy of the Protestant Episcopal Church, which convened at his St. Luke's sanctuary in Washington D.C. Crummell led the motion to change the Conference from an exclusively Negro body to one composed of Church Workers among Colored People, so as to include White clergy as well as Black clergy. The motion was accepted and implemented and the first White members of the body were introduced, those being the Rev. Calbraith B. Perry, then vicar of St. Mary's Chapel in Baltimore, and the Rev. George B. Johnson, Rector of St. James First African Church of Baltimore.[64]

There is no question that the vision of Alexander Crummell to improve the moral, intellectual, economic, and cultural conditions of the Black community in the nineteenth century prepared the way for many of the changes sought for in the twentieth century Civil Rights Movement.  His demand for equality in the Body of Christ is also a cry still heard, but sadly, not always heeded even today.

## THE SLAVE WHO BECAME A BISHOP   (20th Century)

### Henry Beard Delaney (1858-1928 A.D.)

The battle for equality between Black and White believers in Christ, as well as between clergy within the

---

[63] Sydney E. Ahlstrom, " A Religious History of the American People" (New Haven: Yale University Press) p.712.

[64] George Bragg, " Afro-American Church Work and Workers." ( Baltimore: Church Advocate Press)

Episcopal Church, was a long and tiring journey. How obvious it is that the Church in any culture tends to be permeated by the attitudes and social norms of that culture. Black leadership within the Episcopal Church, as well as within all the other denominations, is an inspiring tale of courage and perseverance. One of the key figures in the appointment of Black Bishops is Henry Beard Delaney. Born in Saint Mary's, Georgia in 1858, to a family still enslaved, the Delaneys won their freedom with the Emancipation provided with the conclusion of the Civil War in 1865.

In 1886 Henry Beard Delaney graduated from Saint Augustine's College, a school that was opened in Raleigh, North Carolina in 1867 by the Protestant Episcopal Church to train former slaves as schoolteachers and ministers. Delaney was destined to spend his entire ministry at that campus as a teacher, priest, archdeacon, and finally bishop. He was consecrated on November 21, 1918 at the Chapel of Saint Augustine's College as suffrant bishop for Colored work in the Diocese of North Carolina.

He was the second Black American bishop in history, with Edward Thomas Demby being consecrated as suffrant bishop of Arkansas two months earlier. The story of this achievement is one of dignity in the face of insult. The challenge to the church was reflected in the realities of society after 1865 with the ending of the Civil War. How could the church operate as an integrated community living in a segregated society? The problem is one faced to some degree even today. Integration alone does not guarantee equality.

It is the hearts of men that needs changing even more than ecclesiastical systems. Still, with the ordination of Absalom Jones to the Episcopal priesthood in 1804, the door of possibility had been opened, and other Black clergy found opportunity within the Episcopal Church. In the aftermath of the war many of the leaders in the church did apparently seek for the church to grow without consideration of race. Initially the Episcopal Church was the only religious body led by whites that set the example of absolute equality in the family of Jesus Christ.[65] Opposition, however, was soon to develop.

The Sewanee Conference, composed of Southern Bishops and leading White laity was called on July 25, 1883 at Sewanee, Tennessee on the campus of the University of the South. The purpose of the conference was to arrive at some policy decisions concerning Black Episcopal congregations that were now growing in the South.[66] The group was unanimous in its conclusions, with the exception of the dissenting vote of Bishop Wilmer of Alabama. Their "findings" were that colored people in any diocese were to be segregated under the direction and authority of the diocesan, with such missionary organizations as might be necessary. This became known as the Sewanee Canon, and was presented to the General Convention of 1883, meeting in Philadelphia.

The so-called "Sewanee Canon" was passed by the House of Bishops, but was defeated by the House of Deputies. However, the proposed legislation of the Sewanee Conference, which failed in the National Church, was incorporated into diocesan law in most places of the South. The result was the disenfranchisement of the Black churchman, just as similar laws were passed about the same time by the Southern states to keep the rights of citizenship from the liberated slaves.[67]The reaction of the Black clergy to the Canon was swift.

At the call of Dr. Alexander Crummel of Washington, D.C., they formed a permanent organization to be known as the Conference of Church Workers Among Colored People, a forerunner to the present organization known as the Union of Black Episcopalians. They saw as their chief priority the resisting of canonical segregation as proposed by the Sewanee

---

[65] George Bragg, " History of the Afro-American Group of Episcopla Church" ( Baltimore: Church Advocate Press 1922)

[66] George Bragg, " History of the Afro-American Group in the Episcal Church" ( Baltimore: Church Advocate Press, 1922)

[67] John H. Edwards, " The Episcopal Church and the Black Man in the United States" (unpublished, McQuire Theological College, 1997)

Canon. They carefully avoided discussion of Black bishops, fearing this would lead to the proposal of two permanently segregated bodies with no hope of reconciliation.

The first two Black bishops, James Theodore Holly (1829-1911) and Samuel David Ferguson (1842-1916), both served in African nations overseas. Bishop Holly founded the Anglican Church in Haiti, and Bishop Ferguson served as the Bishop of Liberia. They were in effect missionaries and builders in underdeveloped areas where, in reality, no White candidates were available for the episcopacy. By 1890 the call for Black Episcopal Bishops in the United States was finally heard. Pointing to the success of Bishops Holly and Ferguson as proof that Black men were ready for higher responsibility, an appeal was made for the consecration of Black bishops in America too.[68] The Southern Bishops meeting in 1891 rejected the appeal, but commended the use of archdeacons for Back work. The Conference for Church Workers Among the Colored People continued to call for Black bishops to emerge within the church.

A compromise was finally reached by the General Convention of 1910, which authorized the dioceses for the first time to elect suffrant bishops without the right of succession and without vote in the House of Bishops.[69] Under this system the suffrant Bishop could only serve the Black community and worked under the direct supervision of the local White bishop of the diocese. Even without real authority, Black Episcopalians as symbols of achievement and hard fought progress revered Bishops Demby and Delaney.

---

[68] J. Carleton Hayden, "From Holly to Turner:Black Bishops in the American Succession," (Unpublished Paper, 1988) p.1
[69] Ibid p.3

# AFRICAN METHODIST EPISCOPALS

## THE FIRST BLACK DENOMINATION

### Richard Allen (1760-1831 A.D.)

**Figure 7**

Richard Allen was born on February 14, 1760 in Philadelphia, Pennsylvania, the slave of a Quaker by the name of Benjamin Chew.  He was sold to a Methodist man near Dover, Delaware while a teenager, and never saw his family again.  His autobiography was found in a trunk after his death in 1831.[70]  While in his teenage years Allen put his faith in Christ for his salvation and joined the Methodist Church. Due to his hard work for his master he was allowed to work for extra pay, which he used ultimately to buy his freedom

For a time Allen traveled as a circuit preacher in New Jersey, Pennsylvania, and Maryland, proclaiming the Gospel message as he traveled from place to place. In February 1786, Allen came to Philadelphia and preached at the 5:00 AM service at St. George's Methodist Church. The service went very well and as he continued to preach at this early hour each Sunday for several weeks, the group of Black worshippers

---

[70]  Milton C. Schaff, " African American Religious History : A Documentary Witness" ( Durham, North Carolina: Duke University Press 1985) p. 135

grew to forty-two. Sometimes Allen would preach up to five times a day in a variety of locations around the city wherever he could gather a group.[71] He finally decided that a place of worship just for Black believers was necessary, but he found much resistance among the white leadership of St. George's Church.

Allen nevertheless continued his preaching ministry, and the number of Black Christians attending the church grew to the point that the ushers had them standing around the walls. The building of a balcony in the church was a direct result of the growth of the Black members. The sad event mentioned previously in this chapter, of the Black believers being banished to the very back of the new gallery, to the area where men still bound in slavery had to sit, was the final insult, and the entire Black portion of the congregation walked out, with Abslom Jones and Richard Allen leading the way.

In 1793, six years after walking out of the St. George's Methodist Church, Allen was able to purchase an old blacksmith shop and convert it into a church, naming it First Bethel Church for Negro Methodists, which was the first place of worship owned by Africans in America. Bishop Francis Asbury came to the church in July 1794 to preach the opening service, and to ordain Allen as a Methodist deacon, the first Black man to be so honored. The church was initially part of the Methodist fellowship, but tensions with the White clergy to control the affairs of the congregation reached a peak in 1814 with a battle in the local courts, which ruled in favor of Allen and the Bethel Church.

As a direct result of the jurisdictional dispute with the White Methodists, the first General Conference of the African Methodist Episcopal Church (AME) was called in 1816 in Philadelphia, and the first Black denomination in America was formed, with Richard Allen becoming its first Bishop. Twenty years later the AME denomination had about seventy-

---

[71] Richard Allen, ' The Life and Times of the Rt. Reverend Richard Allen ( Philadelphia: Martin and Boston Pub. 1833)

hundred members, and about three times that many by
In the meantime it had founded the first Negro magazine
America (1841), and acquired Wilberforce University in Ohio
(1856).[72]  The Mother Bethel Church, as it came to be called,
led the way in calling for an end to slavery, sheltering runaway
slaves, and planting AME churches in other parts of
Pennsylvania and surrounding states.

In a 1984 survey by Ebony Magazine it was stated that
there are between eighteen to twenty million nominal Black
Christians in the United States.  Of America's professing Black
Christians about eighty percent belong to denominations
founded and controlled by Blacks.  Thus is the legacy of
Richard Allen, one of dignity and self-determination for Black
Christians.  It is significant to note, however, that since its
founding the AME church has never practiced institutional
racism, but has always opened its doors to people of all
backgrounds, applying the creed that, "God is our Father;
Christ Our Redeemer; Man our Brother."[73]

---

[72] Sydney E. Ahlstrom, " A Religious History of the American People" ( New
Haven: Yale University Press 1972)p.708.

[73] Milton C. Sernett, " African American Religious History : A Documentary
Witness" ( Durham North Carolina: Duke University Press 1985)

# THE PENTECOSTAL MOVEMENT OF THE 20TH CENTURY

## THE ONE-EYED PREACHER WHO LAUNCHED A WORLDWIDE MOVEMENT

### William Joseph Seymour (1855-1922 A.D.)

The fastest growing branch of the Christian church around the world today is that of Pentecostal believers. The theology of Pentecostalism is based on a literal interpretation of the Bible as the Word of God. The distinctiveness of Pentecostal teaching is found in the belief in divine healing made available in the atonement of Christ on the cross, the possibility of miracles even today, and the speaking in unknown tongues as an ecstatic expression of one's having been filled with the Holy Spirit.

At the turn of the twentieth century there was not a single American Pentecostal Church denomination anywhere. Today, however, Pentecostalism has spread across the American church landscape and virtually around the world. Some of its fundamental beliefs are found in all mainline churches including: Roman Catholic, Methodist, Lutheran, Episcopalian and Baptist.

A 1980 Gallup Poll, published in the Christianity Today Magazine, highlighted this astounding growth. The poll indicated that 19 percent of the total population of the United State, or about 50 million people, identified themselves as Pentecostal or Charismatic Christians. This phenomenal growth is one of the main reasons that Harvard theologian Harvey Cox has stated that Pentecostalism is "reshaping religion in the twenty-first century."[74]

---

[74] Edward Hyatt, " Two Thousand Years of Charismatic Christianty" ( Hyatt International Ministries Pub. 1996) p. 3

What is not so well known is the fact that this world wide movement which now embraces every nationality and every continent, began in a small Black church located at 312 Azusa Street in Los Angeles, California called the Apostolic Faith Mission, under the leadership of a Black American minister, William Joseph Seymour.  Unheralded and often overlooked by some possibly because of his racial heritage, William Joseph Seymour is, nevertheless, the "father of modern-day Pentecostalism."[75]

The exact date of Seymour's birth is uncertain, but it appears to have been around 1855.  Historians believe he was born in rural Louisiana, and both he and his parents were slaves.  By the end of the Civil War and the emancipation of slaves in the south, he would have been around 12 years old. Somehow in those developmental years he lost one eye and had it replaced with a glass one.

Seymour apparently moved to Texas as a young man and became involved in ministry with the Baptist church and possibly at some point with the AME fellowship as well.  It was there also that he came in contact with a small group of Black Christians known as the "Evening Light Saints" which was part of the so called Holiness Movement, an offshoot of the Methodists who sought to retain the original emphasis of John Wesley. They taught the necessity of a born again experience or conversion, evidenced by a holy life. They also taught that there was a second experience necessary for final salvation, known as holiness or entire sanctification.  William Seymour became convinced of the truthfulness of this doctrine and became a preacher for the Evening Light Saints.[76]

---

[75] Burkett Newman, "Black Apostles," (Boston: G.K. Hall and Co., 1978) p.216

[76] Ibid p.218

# Rev. William Joseph Seymour

**Figure 8**

It was in Houston that another significant encounter would bring change to Seymour's life. He joined the Bible School of Charles Parham. The school was teaching a new doctrine concerning the baptism of the Holy Spirit. Parham was a former Methodist minister from Kansas, where he had run a small communal Bible School in 1898.  The students were not charged tuition, but were required to "live by faith."  In January 1901, one of Parham's students, an eighteen-year-old girl named Agnes Ozman, was baptized in the Holy Spirit, and began to speak in other tongues as the Spirit gave utterance. Parham constructed his thesis that glossolalia (tongues) was the Biblical evidence of being baptized in the Holy Spirit.[77]  The Parham's moved to Texas and began a similar Bible School in Houston 1905.

To skirt the Jim Crow Laws they allowed Seymour and other Blacks to study at the school by putting them in the room next door to the classroom and leaving the door open so that the Black students could hear what was being taught. In 1906 an invitation for Seymour to move to Los Angeles, California and pastor a Nazarene Church was extended. Seymour's tenure as pastor lasted merely one day. Because he preached in the Sunday morning service this new doctrine of the baptism of the Holy Spirit, by the evening service, the church leaders had put a pad lock on the door.

Moving into the home of sympathetic friends, Mr. and Mrs. Lee at 312 Lee Street in Los Angelos, an evening prayer meeting and Bible study service were started. Many people began to come each night for prayer and to seek this experience of the in filling of the Holy Spirit.  Finally on April 9, 1906 the experience that Seymour had been proclaiming became a reality.  While Sister Farrar and another friend from Houston were at the home of the Lee's eating dinner something incredible happened.  A description of this encounter is as follows:

> Sister Farrar rose from her seat, walked over to Brother Lee, and said, "The Lord tells me to lay hands on you for the Holy Ghost."  And when she laid her hands on him, he fell out of his chair as though dead, and began to speak in other tongues.  Then they went

---

[77] Frank Bartleman, " Azusa Street" ( Plainfield: Bridge Pub. Inc. 1925)

over to the prayer meeting at Sister Asbury's house. When Brother Lee walked into the house, six people were already on their knees praying.  As he walked through the door, he lifted his hands and began to speak in tongues.  The power fell on the others, and all six began to speak in tongues.[78]

## AZUSA STREET MISSION

### Figure 9

Soon an old abandoned Methodist church, which was being used as a stable, was rented to accommodate the growing crowds. Little did anyone realize that the old Azusa Street Mission would soon become the most talked about spot in the city, and the launching point for a worldwide movement.[79]  From 1906-1909 the revival continued unabated. The initial constituency was of all races and from many

---

[78] Pentecostal Evangel Magazine, 1956 p.

[79] Burkett Newman, "Black Apostles," (Boston: G.K. Hall and Co., 1978)

nations.  Seymour continued as the senior pastor until his death on September 28, 1922 in Los Angeles.[80] Sadly when Rev. Seymour died his heart was broken.  He had believed with all his heart that Pentecost was God's answer to racism in America.  He believed that the Pentecostal church would demonstrate to the world that the work of the Holy Spirit in people's lives would cause them to love their brothers and sisters as themselves, regardless of race or heritage.  He lived long enough to see the initially interracial revival capitulate to the racial separation of the society in his day, and the Pentecostal church bow to racial division.

---

[80] Edward Hyatt, " Two Thousand Years of Charismatic Christianity" ( Hyatt International Ministries Publishers 1996) p. 169

# CHAPTER 9

# THE UNTOLD STORY OF BLACK MISSIONARIES

The enterprise of world missions is very important to me. My wife and I spent sixteen years in cross-cultural missionary endeavors, first in Western Alaska among the Yupik people, but mostly on the continent of Africa. All of our children were born and raised on the mission field. I believe that the commission of Christ to bring the Gospel message to the entire world is just as valid and needed today as it has ever been in world history. However, I was quite amazed at my own ignorance when I discovered after reading an article by Baptist minister Reid Trulson that the first missionaries in American history were not dedicated White Christians, but courageous former slaves.

## The Black Missionary Concept of a Congregational Minister

The idea of training Black Christians as missionaries to Africa was promoted at Newport, Rhode Island by the anti-slavery Congregationalist Pastor, Rev. Samuel Hopkins. In 1773 he and Rev. Ezra Stiles (later President of Yale) solicited support for a plan to send out missionaries; thirty or forty well trained Negroes, "inspired with the spirit of martyrdom." [81]

Hopkins began tutoring free Blacks in theology, encouraging them to consider work as missionaries and began to raise missions' funds for their support. Soon he had sent two prospective missionaries, Bristol Yamma and John Quamine, to Princeton College for Theological training. Then came the American Revolution. John Quamine was killed and

---

[81] Sandy D. Martin, " Black Baptist and African Missions" ( Macon: Mercer University Press 1989)

Hopkins' work was interrupted by the British occupation of Newport. After the war Hopkins unsuccessfully tried to revive the project. Salmur Nubia was to accompany Bristol Yamma to Africa, but funds were no longer available. Attention was focused on building the new nation, and some White Americans debated whether or not Black's could even comprehend the Gospel.[82]

## The First True American Missionary

Meanwhile, John Marrant, a free Black from New York City, was already ministering cross-culturally by preaching to the Indians. As a teenager in Charleston, South Carolina, Marrant had stood outside a church window listening to George Whitefield preach. Moved by the sermon, Marrant gave his life to Christ and began preaching in the Black community. Later he learned the language of an Indian friend and gained access to the Indian tribes in New York State. His ministry led to the conversion of the King of the Cherokees and his daughter.

By 1775 John Marrant had carried the gospel to the Cherokees, Creeks, Catawar, and Housaw Indians. Marrant is apparently the first man in America to share the Gospel with people of another culture, which makes him by definition, our first true missionary.

## The First Black Baptist Congregations

While the Revolutionary War closed the door on Hopkins's plan for Black missionaries, it opened doors elsewhere. When the British captured Savannah in December of 1778, many of the planters who supported the American cause fled. Their abandoned slaves moved into Savannah, where they found freedom behind British lines.

---

[82] Reid Trulson, " The Black Missionaries" ( Downers Grove: Inter-Varsity Press, 1993)

Among the refugees were members of a church in Silver Bluff, South Carolina, which had the first Black Baptist Church in America. Following their Pastor, Rev. David George, they joined the first African Baptist Church in Savannah. This church was founded and pastored by Rev. George Liele, a freed slave who often preached at Silver Bluff before the war.[83]

When the House of Commons signed a declaration of peace in March 1782, the troops in Savannah decided to evacuate. The former slaves knew they would lose their freedom when their protection was gone and the planters returned. George Liele was already struggling with the heirs of his former master who were trying to re-enslave him. The report of the returning planters caused the scattering of the Black Church, is similar to that experience by the church in Jerusalem as recorded in Acts 8: 1- 4.

## America's First Foreign Missionary

Liele, seeking to extend the ministry and preserve his freedom, indentured himself to a British officer, Col. Kirkland. When the British left Savannah late in 1782, Liele and his family sailed with the Colonel to Kingston, Jamaica. By September of 1784 Liele had paid back his indenture and was to devote all his time to preaching. With four other former American slaves he formed the First African Baptist Church of Kingston. He preached to the Jamaican slaves on plantations, at the racecourse, and opened his home for meetings.

Despite persecutions at baptism and meetings, the church grew numerically. Ten years later the membership numbered over five hundred. This early church-planting ministry in Jamaica has led some historians to regard George Liele as America's first foreign missionary. The scattering, which began in Savannah, continued well into the next year as the war slowly wound to a close. When the British left

---

[83] Leory Fitts, " A history of Black Baptsits " ( Boston: Broadman Press 1985)

Charleston in 1782, David George fled to Nova Scotia with some White loyalists and ex-slaves. For the next ten years he ministered to the exiled Blacks in Nova Scotia.

## Taking the Gospel Back Home

It was in 1792 that White English missionary William Carey sailed for India. This venture has been referred to as the beginning of the modern missionary movement. However, by this same time, thousands of former slaves were already immigrating to Africa, and some of them were Christians carrying the Gospel with them. These were not short-term appointments, but rather permanent commitments. It was assumed that a former slave would be immune to African diseases. However, the mortality among Black Americans was as high as it was White Americans.

David George was among the twelve thousand Black settlers who sailed from Nova Scotia to Sierra Leone in 1792. Rev Daniel Coker, an organizer of the African Methodist Episcopal Church, emigrated in 1821 with the first shipload of colonists sent by the American Colonization Society. Although these men ministered primarily among the emigrants, both encouraged African-American missionaries to come to Africa.

David George went to London to secure aid for the Baptist cause in Freetown and Coker wrote to Americans, seeking help for missionaries of all denominations. The colonization society also encouraged the missionaries to emigrate. The presence of Christians among the settlers was considered to be a benefit for the colonies, and the colonization societies solicited funds, claiming they were helping to Christianize Africa. The reality was, however, that like David George and Coker, these missionaries worked not among the interior people, but among the settlers.

# The First American Missionary to Africa

The honor of being the first American to go to Africa as a missionary is generally accorded to the Rev. Lott Carey. Born a slave in Virginia, Carey's life was one of dedication and adventure. As a young man, Carey was hired out by his master to the Shockhoe Tobacco Warehouse in Richmond. He was converted to Christianity while worshipping in a segregated church gallery. His grandmother's name was Mihala. Her dedication to Christ deeply effected Lott's life. When he asked his grandmother if the people back in Africa knew of God's love, she responded almost prophetically by declaring:

> Son, you will grow strong. You will lead man, and perhaps it may be you who will travel over the big seas to carry the great secret to my people. Mihala will be dust, but her prayers will live that your feet will find the path and after you, others of our race, hundreds of them.[85]

Lott Carey soon taught himself to read and write and began to preach. He purchased freedom for himself and his two children by selling waste-tobacco, which he collected from the warehouse floor. His wife had died while still a slave. Soon he was promoted at the warehouse because of his excellent ability to manage and plan. Carey became the pastor of the eight hundred-member African Baptist Church in Richmond, and in 1815 he led in the formation of the Richmond African Baptist Missionary Society. The society was organized for the purpose of sending missionaries to Africa, and by 1821 the contributions from Christian slaves and freedmen totaled seven hundred dollars.

Though a quiet and reserved man, Carey volunteered to be the society's first missionary. He and his second wife

---

[85] J.E. East, " Lotte Carey, Pioneer Missionary" ( Washington D.C. 1965)

were commissioned along with Rev. and Mrs. Collin Teague and their son Hilary. The passion of Carey's heart can best be described only in his own words. When people inquired about his desires to leave the comforts and economic securities of his home in America to go to Africa, According to the writings of Ralph Gurley in 1835, Carey replied:

> I am an African, and in this country, however meritorious my conduct, and respectable my character, I cannot receive credit due to either. I wish to go to a country where I shall be estimated by my merits, not by my complexion; and I feel bound to labor for my suffering race.

In 1821 they sailed for Africa. Carey's final sermon to his congregation in Richmond was both incredibly moving and deeply inspiring. An insert of his final sermon is as follows:

> I am about to leave you and expect to see your faces no more. I long to preach to the poor Africans the way of life and salvation. I don't know what may befall me, whether I may find a grave in the ocean, or among the savage men, or more savage wild beasts on the Coast of Africa; nor am I anxious what may become of me. I feel it my duty to go; and I very much fear that many of those who preach the Gospel in this country, will blush when the Savior calls them to give account of their labors in His cause, and tell them, "I commanded you to go into all the world, and preach the Gospel to every creature; the Savior may ask what have you been doing? Have you endeavored to the utmost of your ability to fulfill the commands I gave you, or have you sought your own gratification, and your own ease, regardless of my Commands?[86]

---

[86] .J.F.A. Ajayi, and Micheal Crowder, " History of West Africa" ( New York: Columbia Press 1973)

Upon arrival in Africa Carey and his team were disappointed to learn that the United States government had not established a free-slave colony, as they had been led to believe, on Sherbo Island off the coast of West Africa. Instead, the group had to travel to live as refugees in the British colony of Sierra Leon. During this period Lott Carey established a mission among the Mandingoes people of the region. Sadly, during his ministry time in Sierra Leon his wife became seriously ill, and was buried in African soil.

Carey moved to the newly established American Colony called Liberia, meaning "place of freedom," in 1825. There his time was devoted to reaching the people of the interior with the message of Christ. At the same time he ministered to the emigrants as the colony's doctor, teacher, pastor and vice-agent. By 1826 Carey had formed a missionary society in connection with his church in Monrovia, the capital city of Liberia. Just two years later, Lott Carey lay dead. He and seven others were killed in a gunpowder explosion as they were making bullets to defend the colony from slave traders. It was a tragic loss of a gifted leader, but Lott Carey's legacy lives on today in the hearts of those who seek to fulfill Christ's Great Commission and live a life of total commitment to Jesus, whatever the cost.

## Black Methodist Missionaries

Generally credited with being the first Methodist Missionary to the American Indians was a freeborn mulatto (part Indian and part Black in heritage) by the name of John Stewart. In September of 1814 the Ohio Conference to the Marietta Circuit appointed Methodist minister Marcus Lindsey. While preaching at a camp meeting in the area a man who had battled with drunkenness and poverty and who seemed intent on committing suicide was wonderfully converted. The man was John Stewart. Immediately Stewart began to attend the Methodist Church in Marietta and soon sensed a call to preach himself, following a sever illness while out in a field in prayer. Here is his account of that day:

> It seemed to me that I heard a voice, like the voice of a woman praising God; and then another, as the voice of a man, saying to me, "You must declare my counsel faithfully[87]

Stewart soon traveled westward determined to share the Gospel with whomever he encountered. He heard of Indians living on a reservation farther north and sensed this was where he must preach. In the area of Sandusky, Ohio Stewart began his ministry among the Wyandotte tribes people. He encouraged Jonathan Pointer, a Black man, to become his interpreter. Freely mixing songs with his exhortations and prayers he soon won many converts, including Pointer, to Christ.

## Jamaican Missionaries Go Forth

Black Christians established other mission societies. George Liele helped to form the Jamaican Baptist Missionary Society to enlist Jamaican Christians for foreign missions. The societies great open door came through the efforts of Thomas Keith. Converted soon after his emancipation in 1833, Keith volunteered to be a missionary to Africa. When no means could be found to finance his travel, Keith decided to get to Africa on his own. Finding a trading ship headed for Africa, Keith signed on as part of the crew and worked his way to his homeland. In West Africa Keith was to proclaim the gospel at the very spot from which he had been stolen years earlier. He sent word to Jamaica that Africans were ready for the missionary work.

---

[87] "The Encyclopedia of World Methodism," Volume II, p. 2251

William Knibb, a White English Missionary in Jamaica, sailed to England to raise money for  support for the Jamaican Missionary Society. Recounting Keith's experience, Knibb told English audiences "fifty thousand Baptists in Jamaica want their fatherland to receive the gospel." The British Baptists responded by opening a mission at Fernando Po.  In 1842 the Jamaican Missionary Society sent out forty-five Black missionaries to work this new station.

Perhaps the character of these men and women is best seen in an incident that occurred in Jamaica in 1842. The forty-five Jamaican missionaries were preparing to leave the Island to take the gospel to Africa when someone asked about their safety. Was it not possible that the very same people they were going to serve might enslave them? One of the missionaries replied; "we have been slaves for men; we can be made slaves for Christ."

# CHAPTER 10

# THE NEGLECT OF SAMARIA

Several years ago I attended a banquet sponsored by Barnabas Ministries in Providence, Rhode Island at the invitation of Founder and Director, Dr. David Wyns. The keynote speaker for the evening was Paul Johanson, President of Elim College in Elmira, New York. Rev. Johanson is a veteran minister of over thirty years of service, having spent some years as a missionary to Kenya in East Africa, the inner city ministry in New York City, and presently as President of Elim College. He opened his message with the following story:

A farmer from northern Minnesota was cutting across a pond on his property while walking home in late winter or early spring. He felt confident the ice was safe as he made his way quickly home, looking forward to the evening meal and a hot cup of coffee. Mid-way across the ice tragedy struck. In seconds the ice beneath him gave way and he plunged into the bitter cold water. As he began to sink he looked to the shore and saw a stranger looking on, apparently a traveler who had stopped to rest and to admire the gray beauty of a quiet winter afternoon in the country.

The stranger sprang into action to reach the desperate farmer. He stayed on his feet for as long as he could and then getting on his belly, he crawled towards the hole in the ice where the farmer was thrashing around, desperately trying to pull himself out of the numbing cold and quickly loosing control of his throbbing limbs. Extending his own coat to the farmer as he crawled towards him, the stranger was extending a lifeline to a man facing certain death. Suddenly the ice cracked in a deafening snap and the stranger too fell into the ice-cold water of the pond.  Willing himself alongside the farmer he looked into his eyes and made a strange request, "tell my wife I love her."  Having said those final words the stranger went beneath the water one last time.  Positioning himself underneath the farmer he placed him on his shoulders, pushed off from the bottom of the relatively shallow pond and with a final burst of strength thrust the farmer from the icy grave and onto solid ice where he now had a chance to live.

The farmer did survive, as a passing neighbor in a pickup truck happened by, saw the drama unfold and rushed the freezing farmer for medical treatment.  The body of the stranger was recovered the following day.  Now the farmer was faced with a plaguing dilemma.  Did he have any responsibility to the man who saved him to do the last thing, he had requested of him, "tell my wife I love her."  The farmer knew that it would be a challenge to learn the identity of the stranger, track down his family, and travel to their home.  To look into the eyes of a grieving widow and to tell her of her husband's final words as he unselfishly gave his life to save his would take great courage of the farmer. He wrestled with his predicament asking himself this question,  Do I have any responsibility to the man who saved my life to do the last thing he requested, tell his wife I love her?

I want to suggest that you and I are faced with the exact same dilemma as that farmer in Northern Minnesota who owed his very life to the sacrificial death of another. The Bible records the final words of Jesus Christ on earth as written by Luke in the first chapter of the Book of Acts, 1:8 as follows:

But you shall receive power after that the Holy Ghost has come upon you and you shall be witness unto me both in Jerusalem, and in Judea and in Samaria and unto the uttermost parts of the earth.

Over the years we who are White Christians in particular have been very focused on being New Testament, and "Great Commission" Christians. Working hard to reach JERUSALEM, our own families, with the message of Jesus Christ to ensure that our families will be saved is a primary focus for most Christians. We who identify with theologically conservative denominations have done quite a fine job in reaching JUDEA, that constituency that lives in our greater community and is of a similar cultural, educational, and ethnic background as ourselves.

Concerning world missions, this is the area that we are most proud of. From the deserts of Africa, to the Arctic regions of Alaska, to the rain forests of South America, missionaries have been sent with the message of the Good News of Christ to the *"uttermost parts of the earth."*

However, I believe with all of my heart, that many White American followers of Jesus Christ are guilty of the **neglect of Samaria.** We are faced with the haunting question of the farmer, "do we have any obligation to the man who saved us to do the last thing he told us?"

## An Overview of Samaria

Samaria in the Bible refers to both a city and a province. Perhaps to conceptualize this  think of New York City, which is in the State of New York. Who were these people called the Samaritans? They were colonists whom the King of Assyria sent to inhabit the Northern Kingdom of Israel after Assyria had conquered Israel and taken away in captivity 27, 280 Jews in 722 BC. Many of the colonists sent to live among the remaining people of Israel were from

Babylon, Hamath, and Arabia, and they continued to practice idolatry in their new home.[88]

With the population of the country diminished by war and captivity, the cultivation of the soil was interrupted. Wild beasts began to multiply and the Lord God used these as His rod of correction. The newcomers concluded that they did not know how to worship the particular god of this country and when they informed the king, he sent them a priest from among the captive Israelites, who took up his residency at Bethel, and began to instruct the people regarding Jehovah, the God of Israel.

He was unable to persuade them to abandon their ancestral idolatry. They erected images of their gods on the high places of the Israelites, and combined their idolatries with the worship of Jehovah. Today we call this syncretism, and have seen the same pattern in world missions in Africa, the Indian population of South America, and particularly in Haiti, with its syncretistic religion of VooDoo, which is a combination of traditional West African spiritual beliefs and Roman Catholicism.

In the days of Jesus a deep hostility existed between the Jews and the Samaritans. The district lay between Galilee and Judea, and at its greatest extent 56 miles long and 47 miles wide. Often Jews traveling between Judea in the south to Galilee in the north would take a much longer route rather then travel through Samaria.[89]

---

[88] J.D. Davis, Davis Dictionary of the Bible 4th Edition, ( Michigan: Baker Book House)

[89] Thoams Whitelaw, " The Preachers Homiletical Commentary" Volume 25 Grand Rapids, Michigan: Baker Book House1978

# SAMARIA IN THE OLD TESTAMENT

According to the Scriptures Samaria was a city built by an evil king, his treacherous son, and wicked daughter-in-law (Kings 16:23-25; 28; 30-31).

> v.23-24 In the thirty first year of Asa king of Judah, Omri became king of Israel, and he reigned twelve years, six of them in Tirzah. He bought the hill of Samaria from Shemer for two talents of silver (about $3800) and built a city on the hill calling it Samaria, ('place of watch') ...

Note that the nation had divided after the death of King Solomon, with the 10 Tribes of the North now being called Israel, and the two tribes of the south being called Judah.

> v. 25 ...But Omri did evil in the eyes of the Lord and sinned even more than those before him.
>
> v 28 Omni rested with his fathers and was buried in Samaria. And Ahab his son succeeded him as king...
>
> v. 29... and he reigned over Israel twenty-two years. Ahab son of Omri did more evil in the eyes of the Lord then any of those before him. He not only considered it trivial to commit the sins of Jeroboam...but he also married Jezebel daughter of Ethbaal king of the Sidonians and began to serve Baal and worship him.

Baal was a sun god, exhibiting different aspects of solar energy, the center of whose worship was Phonecia. Lascivious rites accompanied the worship of Baal, the sacrifice of children in the fire by parents, and kissing the image. Jehovah expressly forbade such idolatrous worship to those who served Him.

## Converted...But Not Entirely

The Book of II Kings 17: 24-40 tells the story of the colonists sent to Samaria by the King of Assyria and their desire to learn how to worship the god of that land. One of the priests who had been exiled from Bethel came to live in Samaria and taught the people how to worship the Lord. Please note that the Israelites had been taken into captivity only by God's permission because of their constant idolatrous ways. Now one of the priests who had failed to convince the Jews to worship God faithfully, was going to try to get these idolatrous foreigners to do what the covenant people of Jehovah had stubbornly refused to do!

> v. 33 They worshipped the Lord, but they also served their own gods in accordance with the customs of the nations from which they had been brought.
> v. 40 They would not listen but persisted in their former practices.  Even while these people were worshipping the Lord, they were serving their idols.  To this day their children and grandchildren continue to do as their fathers did.

This inclination to retain our idolatrous practices even after an alleged conversion is still common today.  When did Christians stop believing that it is imperative that we must indeed give up our old habits, our old hatreds, old prejudices that have become like idols in our hearts when we decide to follow Christ? Where did the belief that we might retain our old idols, and still please the Lord? That we do not have to have to change on a deep fundamental level in order to serve the God of the Bible is completely unscriptural.

## SAMARIA IN THE NEW TESTAMENT

### A People <u>Scorned</u> By Man

The Book of Ezra records the captive Jews finally returning after some 70 years of captivity to rebuild the Temple in Jerusalem under the leadership of Zerubbabel. When the workers came to begin the task the Samaritans of the region offered to assist, in that by now over the years there had been much intermarriage between the colonists and the local Israelites. The pure blood Jews of the Diaspora refused the offer, in that the Samaritans were neither of pure Hebrew blood nor of uncontaminated worship. In response, the Samaritans ultimately built their own temple to worship Jehovah on Mount Gerazim in their region. This rival Temple was destroyed in 129 B.C. by the Jewish warrior John Hyracanus, but the Samaritans continued to offer their adorations on the summit of the hill where the sacred edifice had stood. They were still doing this when Jesus Christ was on the earth, as was referred to in John 4:20,21.

### A People <u>Loved</u> by Christ

I think it is of significance to note, that a minority so hated by the Jews in the days of Jesus that when they referred to them they spat out in contempt the words, '*Samaritan dogs,*' and reviled that they would not pass through their community, were of great concern to Christ. Jesus, by word and example, showed only respect, compassion, and love for these rejected people, who centuries before had been forcibly removed from their homeland and taken to this land so far away. Notice the example used by Jesus in several passages of Scripture:

103

**The Story of the Samaritan Woman.** John 4: 3-42 (A few key verses):

> v. 3 He left Judea (in the south) and departed again to Galilee (in the north)
>
> v. 4 And He must needs go through Samaria.
>
> v. There came (to the well) a woman of Samaria to draw water: Jesus said unto her, Give me a drink (or let me share your cup)
>
> v. Then said the woman of Samaria to him, how is it that you, being a Jew, ask for a drink from me, a woman of Samaria?  For the Jews have no dealings with the Samaritans.

Jesus goes on to tell the woman of Living Water in v. 13 that can quench the very thirst of man's soul. He tells her plainly He is the promised Messiah in v. 25-26, and He stays in the city of Samaria for two full days, sleeping in their homes, eating at their tables, drinking from their cups, and teaching them eternal truth. The Samaritans then drew their own conclusion:

> v.  42 ...ourselves and we know that this man really is the Savior of the world.

**The Ministry to the Ten Lepers.** Luke 17: 12-18 tells us:

> Now on his way to Jerusalem, Jesus traveled along the border between Samaria and Galilee.  As he was going into a village, ten men who had leprosy met him.  They stood at a distance and called out in a loud voice, "Jesus, Master, have mercy on us!
>
> When he saw them, he said "Go show yourselves to the priests."  And as they went they were cleansed.

One of them, when he saw he was healed, came back, praising God in a loud voice.  He threw himself at Jesus' feet and thanked him…and he was a Samaritan.

Jesus asked, "Were not all ten cleansed?  But where are the nine? Was no one found to return and give praise to God except this foreigner?"  Then he said to him, "Rise and go, your faith has made you whole."

Please note that suffering and disease had forged an alliance between nine Jewish lepers and one Samaritan, who were all suffering the same fate.  They were all together in their hopeless condition.  How tragic that only in times of war or tragedy are we prepared to set aside our prejudices. How amazing also to note, that only this hated Samaritan turned back to thank Christ when the miracle of healing took place. How quickly we are inclined to take God for granted after a time of blessing!

Finally, we read the Parable of the Good Samaritan in Luke 10: 25-37. You cannot understand the full significance of this most famous parable of Jesus, until you read it in its context and understand whom the hearer was.

v. 25 on one occasion an expert in the law (of Moses) stood up to test Jesus.  "Teacher," he asked, "what must I do to inherit eternal life?"  "What is written in the Law?" Jesus replied.  "How do you read it?"  He answered:  "Love the Lord your God with all your heart and with all your soul and with all your strength and with all your mind, and Love your neighbor as yourself."  "You have answered correctly," "Do this and you will live."  But he wanted to justify himself, so he asked Jesus, "And who is my neighbor?"

It is the reply to this question by an extremely religious man who sensed something incomplete in his own relationship with God, and he wanted to justify himself. When Jesus spins the tale of the Jew traveling home from the temple in Jerusalem to Jericho and being beaten by robbers and left to die, he had the man's attention. Jesus continues and tells of two religious leaders coming upon the scene on their way home to Jericho, where the priests resided when not on temple duty. These men were in too much of a hurry to get involved with the suffering even of a fellow Jew, possibly a fellow priest, so they hurried on. He tells of other religious travelers that also come upon the injured man and after taking a close look at him, also move on to more important business. The teacher of the law must have gasped in horror as the hero who emerges in the story is a hated Samaritan, who stops, inconveniences himself, treats the wounded man on the spot, invests his own money to help a stranger who if healthy, would have called him a dog.

To Jesus final question in v. 36 "Which of these do you think was a neighbor to the man who fell into the hands of robbers?" The expert in the Law replied, "The one who had mercy upon him." Jesus told him, "Go and do likewise." The example of Jesus would clearly lead us to conclude two things; Firstly, that we are to care for all our neighbors, and demonstrate mercy and compassion by our deeds, not just platitudes of righteousness only with our words. Secondly, that the most loathsome form of prejudice in the nostrils of God is that which emanates from the heart of a religious person.

## SAMARITANS AMONG US
### Clarifying the Metaphor

I am using the term Samaritan today to refer to those minority communities that live in our midst. In America this would refer to Native Americans, Hispanics, Asians, and the largest minority group of all, the African-Americans. For the sake of this writing, let us focus on the Black community.

# A Review of African-American History

A brief chronology would be summarized as approximately 300 years of slavery; 12 years of Reconstruction; 100 years of Segregation, and 30 years of Affirmative Action.  As explained previously, racism, the dehumanizing of African peoples based on their skin color, was simply an ideology created to justify economic exploitation. Between 1501 and 1870 nearly 12 million Africans were forcibly loaded aboard ships on the West Coast of Africa and taken to the Americas. On the sides of many of these ships were the words *JESU CHRISTO.* Once economic motives supported racism, it quickly became the law of the land and Biblical rationalization was also sought to justify this tragedy!

## The Response of the Church... *Tolerance of Injustice*

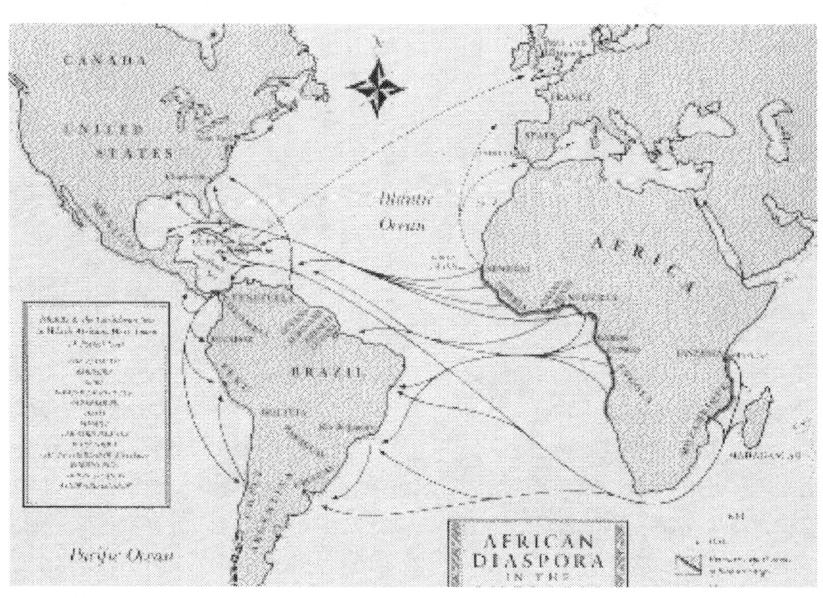

Figure 10

The response of the Christian church in this newly developing "Christian Nation" was largely compliance. Initially slaves were not allowed to hear the Gospel because British Law declared that once a slave became a Christian he must be set free. In the 1700's Maryland and Virginia passed laws to the effect that Christian baptism did not confer freedom upon slaves.

The real breakthrough in the evangelization among slaves came during the Great Awakening led by Jonathan Edwards and George Whitefield in the mid-1700's. Tragically the demand for cotton consequently increased the demand for slave labor in the South. Despite the tremendous restrictions placed on just about every aspect of the slaves' lives there was a certain degree of freedom allowed by the White masters in their religious worship. The irony was that these same masters who might whip a slave on Saturday, always found themselves in church on Sunday, and lived oblivious to this incredible contradiction.

## 18th Century...IN THE NORTH, *THE SEPARATE ALTAR*

Of America's professing African-American Christians, about 80 percent belong to denominations founded and controlled by Blacks. Despite all the societal efforts made to ensure that the Blacks and Whites would work and study together, the races largely continue to worship in segregation.

## 19th Century ...IN THE SOUTH, *THE CIVIL WAR*

The Civil War split the nation. This was the most bitter conflict in American History. The source of the conflict between the North and the South resulted from fundamentally different ways of life. Economy in the South was heavily based on agricultural and growing cotton. The North was heavily industrialized and factories and manufacturing were central to their economy. Growing and harvesting cotton required large numbers of workers. This workforce was made up of about four million slaves.

By the 1800's there was a large move in the North to see slavery, which was now illegal, totally abolished in the South. The South feared that losing slaves would have severe economic repercussions. When President Lincoln was elected in 1860 on a platform that opposed slavery, seven Southern states seceded from the Union. They formed the Confederate States of America. On April 12, 1861, Southern Confederate forces captured Fort Sumter in South Carolina.

**Figure 11**

The Civil War consisted of more than 50 major battles and 5,000 minor battles. In less than five years, more than 600,000 men were killed and hundreds of thousands of others were wounded. The Union Army, with more soldiers and resources eventually overcame the Confederate Army. On April 9, 1865, General Lee surrendered his Confederate Troops and the war was over. Five days after the surrender treaty was signed, a Southern sympathizer, John Wilkes Booth, assassinated President Abraham Lincoln.

## 20th Century ... ACROSS AMERICA, *CIVIL RIGHTS*

Just because slavery ended in 1865 with the ending of the Civil War, this did not mean that freedom and equality were the same thing. Following the Civil War was the period of Reconstruction. Reconstruction, which lasted from 1865 to 1877, during which time African Americans made major political and social gains especially with the passing of the Fourteenth Amendment in 1868 guaranteeing citizenship, due process, and equal protection under the law. The Fifteenth Amendment in 1870 brought political empowerment, giving Blacks the right to vote on the same basis as Whites; universal male suffrage.

However, by 1877 Northern White Republicans abandoned the Reconstruction experiment, and African Americans saw many of their hard-won gains quickly evaporate. The agenda for genuine equality would have to wait nearly another century again before becoming a national issue. Reconstruction led to segregation which only came to an end legally with the 1954 Brown vs. Board of Education decision that declared that "separate but equal" education for Blacks and Whites was separate, but in no way was it equal. In 1955 Rosa Parks refused to give up her seat on the bus, and the Montgomery Bus Boycott was launched, ending segregation on public transport. Many challenges followed, as this brief glimpse of key events suggests:

- In 1960 Sit In at Woolworth's in Greensboro, NC
- 1961 Freedom Rides
- 1962 Mississippi Riots
- 1963 Birmingham Alabama March
- 1965 Selma Alabama March
- 1965 President Johnson signs Voting Rights Act
- 1968 Dr. Martin Luther King Assassinated in Memphis
- 1970's School Busing to Integrate Public Schools
- 1980's Growth of Affirmative Action
- 1990's Decline of Affirmative Action

Figure 12

As a close friend of mine Allen Green once said, while discussing this painful subject, "Racism compromises the Gospel of Jesus Christ to its very core!" I could not agree more completely, nor have said it more clearly. Racism in the world is completely understandable if we accept man's nature as sin, being inherited from Adam. Racism in the hearts of Christians, on the other hand, is totally unacceptable as it is the ultimate contradiction to everything that Jesus taught and demonstrated.

During the 18th Century, the White Christian church allowed the separate altar. In the 19th Century, many White Christians justified slavery by distorting Scripture. In the 20th Century, many White Christians looked the other way when Black brothers and sisters in Christ were beaten and even killed, as they sought the rights legally guaranteed to every citizen in Christian America. In many cases the White church congregations fled the inner cities as minorities moved in, thus abandoning and incredible field of service.

At the same time that millions of dollars are invested each year in foreign mission enterprises, many look from the relative safety of the suburbs at the violence and deterioration of the inner cities with a critical attitude, forgetting that it is the church that left the city, and now takes no responsibility for the results. As we enter the 21st Century, it is long past time that the Christian church lead by example in bringing about genuine oneness in the Body of Christ. Listen to what the Bible says:

> II Corinthians 5:14-18 that, Christ's love compels us, because we are convinced that one died for all…and he died for all that those who live should no longer live for themselves but for him who dies for them and was raised again. So from now on we regard no one from a worldly point of view. Though we once regarded Christ this way, we do so no longer. Therefore, if any man be in Christ he is a new creation, the old is gone,

the new has come.   All this is from God, who reconciled us to Himself through Christ and *gave unto us the ministry of reconciliation.*

Colossians 3:11 Here (in Christ) there is neither Greek nor Jew, circumcision nor uncircumcision, barbarian, Scythian, slave or free, but Christ is all and is in all.

Racial reconciliation, therefore, is the responsibility of the Church, and it must begin in the Church.   It is not primarily a political, social, psychological, or economic issue. It is a spiritual issue, and the issue simply stated, is sin. The only antidote for sin, according to the Bible, is repentance.   The answer to the farmers' dilemma in the story above is affirmative.  The answer to the Christian's dilemma is affirmative too.   We **do** have an obligation to the Man who saved us to do the last thing he told us, tell the entire world, Jerusalem, Judea, **and Samaria,** that God loves them.  We must not just say it with words, but validate it with action.

# CHAPTER 11

# ONE BRICK AT A TIME

It is essential in the process of dealing with social, spiritual or individual problems to first identify the root causes, and then after careful consideration and study, to seek solutions. In the final chapter of this book I would like to consider some very practical steps that can be implemented in order to dismantle the wall of racial separation in our society at large, but more specifically, in the church community.

In the Fall of 1997, the Promise Keepers organization held a rally on the Mall in Washington D.C. A million Christian men from around America traveled to our nation's capitol for this historic occasion. A colleague of mine at Saint Augustine's College, Mr. Don Donaldson, who is the director of academic computer services, accompanied me and eight of our young Christian men to Washington to be a part of this gathering for prayer and national repentance.

The challenge of the various speakers, which included Jack Hayford, Tony Evans, and John Perkins, strongly addressed the issue of racial prejudice and insensitivity over the years in the Body of Christ in America. How thrilling it was to hear nearly a million men sing in unison such classic hymns as, "How Great Thou Art", and "Amazing Grace." How moving it was to see men of various races and denominational backgrounds join hands in prayer and embrace in brotherhood.

Several hours into the event a television cameraman approached our group. Possibly seeing us all wearing sweatshirts with the name of our college, or possibly because seeing a White man with a group of nine Black men caught his eye. He asked if he could interview me and ask a few questions, and I agreed. The interaction went something like this:

Reporter:  Do you really think this event will make any lasting impact on the racial divisions in the American church and in American society?

My Response: I do not believe that the wall of racial separation that exists in our nation and even in our churches will fall like the wall at Jericho, just because we shout at it. This wall has been under construction for nearly 300 years and it is very high, too high to climb.  This wall extends to all sections of our country, so it is too wide to go around.  I think the only way to dismantle this wall is ONE BRICK AT A TIME.  There are nearly one million men here today and each man has two hands.  I do indeed believe we can make a major dent in that wall if we all do our part, one brick at a time.

In that brief and spontaneous response, I summarized, what is for me the heart of the issue.  It is everybody's job to be intentionally engaged in dismantling the wall of ignorance regarding race in America.  Following are several models to consider in approaching this endeavor.

## SUGGESTED MODELS AND MINSTRIES

There are three God-ordained institutions in society; the family, civil government, and the church.  It is in ones family of origin that many of our attitudes and beliefs about race are formed.  For some this is a wonderful environment of growth and development.  For others the prejudices of our parents become internalized and become our prejudices too. Civil government has a mixed record on civil rights for all its citizens, particularly the harsh realities of the past where even the Supreme Court in the nineteenth century declared Blacks to be counted as two-thirds of a man.

Only the church has the mandate and the power to address this issue successfully. The question is do we have the inclination?  Below are several models of those who do have the inclination to do something practical, positive, and constructive relative to the issue of racial healing in our nation, and in the Church of Jesus Christ.

## [PAR] PASTORS FOR AWAKENING AND RECONCILLIATION

This is a cooperative fellowship of clergy in the Greater Raleigh, North Carolina community who have been meeting together since 1996.    They gather the second Tuesday morning of each month 8:00 A.M.-9: 30 AM, rotating to different churches each month.    A cross-section of denominations are involved, and the composition is truly multi-racial.  Coffee and refreshments are served, followed by a time of fellowship, prayer, and occasionally a devotional.

An annual prayer retreat has also been held out of the city each year, giving a wonderful time of uninterrupted interaction and relationship building between clergy.  The clergy have also joined hands together for a number of joint ventures listed below:

- In April 1997 PAR brought Texas pastor, author and evangelist Tony Evans to Raleigh for a conference on Racial Healing.  Several thousand people of various racial and denominational backgrounds attended.

- In June 1998 the clergy banned together under the leadership of pastor Michael Stewart of First Assembly of God Church in Raleigh, North Carolina to conduct a project called CONVOY OF HOPE.    After months of preparation 700 volunteers from 22 churches traveled to Chavis Park, located in a low-income neighborhood in the southeast section of the city. During the course of the day 35,000 pounds of groceries were given away to over 3,000 local residents. A number of tents were set up to provide free medical screening for such diseases as diabetes and high blood pressure. The medical staff was all volunteers, headed up by a surgeon from Duke Medical Center. A Gospel tent area was also very active as seven different pastors and local choirs participated in this joyous event. Special activities for children including clowns, pony rides, a basketball exhibition by a former Harlem Globetrotter and a chance to hear the message of Jesus' love shared with them.

- As a result of the tireless efforts of Don Rayon, director of the Raleigh Area Concerts of Prayer, a project was organize entitled PRAY RALEIGH '99. A registration form was developed and churches enlisted to ADOPT A BLOCK. The strategy is for churches from across the Greater Raleigh area to adopt one block in the inner city and commit to pray for the people there daily but also to contact and develop a relationship with a pastor in that community and seek to find practical ways to assist him and his congregation. What a tremendous way for the Body of Christ in the suburbs, to build meaningful relationships with fellow believers in parts of the city they seldom if ever see. It is too early to tell how fruitful this venture will be but the early indications are very encouraging.

# PAR GUIDELINES

## Purpose

*To promote racial, ethnic, and denominational reconciliation among pastors in the Greater Raleigh area by serving Jesus Christ together to demonstrate biblical unity.*

## Commitments

*Intentional*

Committed to become proactive in the pursuit of racial and ethnic reconciliation, personally taking the initiative without waiting for others to move first.

*Sensitive*

Committed to develop spiritual discernment and racial sensitivity in order to avoid saying or doing anything, which might be racially or ethnically offensive.

*Persistent*

Committed to follow through persistently in all of these commitments and never give up the pursuit of racial and ethnic reconciliation regardless of what others do.

*Gracious*

Committed to giving others the benefit of the doubt when they err or fail to act according to expectations.

*Teachable*

> Committed to learning as much as possible about the unique character and cultural distinctive of other racial and ethnic groups in the body of Christ in order to gain an appreciation for their special place in God's design.

*Relational*

> Committed to building Christ-centered relationships with people from different racial and ethnic backgrounds in order to model the fellowship of the Spirit in the bond of love.

Should you be interested in more information as to how to develop a similar clergy association as Pastors for Awakening and Reconciliation  (PAR) in your city you can contact:

> Raleigh-Area Concerts of Prayer
> 1403 Suterland Road
> Cary, NC 27511

## THE NATIONAL JOBS PARTNERSHIP

One of the most exciting and successful ministries that I am aware of that is indeed dismantling the wall of racial separation began in Raleigh in 1996 as The Jobs Partnership of Raleigh, and now has rapidly spread to other communities in other states.   In one of those sovereign coincidence the owner of a local construction company had lunch with a local inner-city  pastor and by the time the check was paid a new ministry had been born.

Reverend Donald McCoy had hired the C.C. Mangum Company to pave the parking lot of his Pleasant Hill UCC Church.  While the project was underway, Chris Mangum, the firms' executive vice president, met Pastor McCoy.  The two men shared a common faith in Christ, and over lunch, Mr. Mangum mentioned his need for employees and the pastor mentioned the number of people in his congregation in need of employment.

The idea of helping each other meet their needs seemed logical. Realizing that other business and churches faced the same situation before them the men agreed to go back to their respective communities and find 12 others to form a partnership of businesses and churches with a common mission of reaching out to, mentoring, training, and employing their unemployed and under-employed neighbors in Raleigh. Within a few weeks each man had successfully recruited 12 other participants to join together and form The Jobs Partnership of Raleigh. A steering committee of eight pastors of different denominations and racial backgrounds, along with seven leaders of diverse businesses formed the committee.

In just the first three years of its existence this joint effort of Christian businessmen and local churches has touched the lives of hundreds of people, and made giant strides towards making a practical contribution to diffusing racial mistrust. A two-fold curriculum was developed to impart basic workplace skills and ethics and the necessary tools to get and keep a job. The "Keys to Personal and Professional Success" courses build on a religious foundation and leads students through a 12-part series of weekly studies on topics that have immediate application in the work- place. Completion of this course is required for job placement.

Over 200 students have successfully completed the program and found good jobs since the first class was held in 1996. The concept of Jobs Partnership has spread to other cities across America as people have seen the many benefits of businesses and churches working together to address the issue of unemployment in their communities.

Presently there are Job Partnerships in: Spartanburg, SC; Chattanooga, TN; Knoxville, TN; Richmond, VA;

Washington, DC; Brenham, TX; Milwaukee, WI; Fresno, CA; Baltimore, MD; Oxford, Edenton, and Henderson, NC. In addition several other cities are in the formation process, including Los Angeles, CA; Chicago, IL; Grand Rapids, MI; St. Louis, MO; Greenville, SC; Dallas TX; and Miami, FL.

Should any reader of this section have interest in starting a Jobs Partnership in your community please contact:

> The National Jobs Partnership
> Executive Director Skip Long
> 4208 Six Forks Road
> Building 2, Suite 320
> Raleigh, NC 27609

## THE SURPRISE BLESSINGS OF REFORM

On August 16, 1999 Time Magazine ran an article entitled, *Welfare: The Undeserving Poor?* The subtitle was *Who Should Still Be On Welfare?* The essence of the article was the fact that although the welfare rolls have dropped almost 50% over the last six years there are still millions of people who have not been able to find there way into meaning full employment. What are some creative ways our communities can deal with this dilemma? A secondary article in the story addresses this issue. It was written by Nancy Gibbs and is entitled, "The Surprise Blessings of Reform."

The story tells of the former Republican Governor of South Carolina, David Beasley, challenging local civil activist Lisa Van Riper to develop a program to assist the states new work requirements for welfare recipient's stick. Armed with determination, creativity, and $200,000 of private money left over from the Governors inaugural, Van Riper went to work persuading every church, synagogue, and civic group in the state to adopt one family on welfare and guide them towards independence.

Today her private foundation, Putting Families First, has become a national model. Nearly 900 groups statewide, including a variety of churches from various theological distinctions, have signed-on to help hundreds of families. The public-private partnership has contributed to a 65% drop in state welfare rolls, but has had other benefits that could not be predicted.

> As white churches work with black families and black churches adopt white families, suspicions float away. "I've been in government for 25 years," says Leon Love, deputy director of community services for the state, "and no program has done as much for race relations as this one has. We didn't go into this with that goal, but these relationships develop based on people, not color. People get to know people, and then it's hard to hate a friend"[90] [Gibbs, p.26].

How encouraging to read in one of our nations most popular secular magazines that people of faith, as well as people of simple good will, when working together in a caring relationship with people of different races cannot only succeed in reaching a goal, but can also build meaningful relationships, and take one more brick out of the wall of racial misunderstanding.

How very possible it is for churches in every community in America to embrace this simple model of adopting even one family on welfare, possibly a single mom and her children, and providing through the loving example of our Lord, the practical assistance that validates our faith through loving acts of service.

---

[90] Nancy Gibbs, "The Surprise Blessings of Reform," Time Magazine, August 16, 1999 Vol. 154, p. 26

# SERIOUS QUESTIONS TO CONSIDER

For those who are willing to seriously consider the problem of racial separation and injustice that is part of our American heritage, I challenge you to consider the following five questions seriously [http://ethics.acusd.edu]. They are adopted from a questionnaire developed by Dr. Lawrence Hinman of the University of Southern California, author of numerous textbooks on Ethics and Philosophy. These questions are as follows:

1.  What is the actual state of American society in regard to race and ethnicity? What are the three most important issues in regard to race and ethnicity today?

2.  What are the minimal conditions necessary for a just society in regard to race and ethnicity? List at least three characteristics or conditions.

3.  What are the ideal conditions necessary for a just society in regard to race and ethnicity? List at least three characteristics or conditions.

4.  How should we get from the actual state to the minimally acceptable state? List specific ways of getting from the actual state of society, to the minimal conditions listed above.

5.  How should we get from the actual state to the ideal state? List specific ways of getting from the actual state of society to the ideal conditions listed above.

These five questions can be a wonderful beginning of meaningful dialogue and interaction on a subject that has been a constant source of division in our nation for some 300 years. They can act as a catalyst to provoke critical thinking at a level that many have never dared to enter before.

## PERSONAL INTERSPECTION AND COMMITMENTS

Beyond the act of deeply considering the matter of race and ethnicity in society at large, let us consider some challenging commitments put forth by the Victoria Holocaust Remembrance and Education Society under the title, "How to Eliminate Racism."

I        **"I will understand what racism is."**

*Racism is a learned behavior.*

1.   It stems from:

- An erroneous belief that we inherit intelligence, behavioral, and cultural, and psychological characteristics along with our physical features;

- Fear due to misinformation and a preconceived notion of others;

- A feeling of superiority to others; and,

- A combination of prejudice and power.

2.   Racism results in:

- Actions or practices, which discriminate against, subordinates, or harasses individuals or groups because of physical features (mostly color of skin), culture and religion.

- Verbal, emotional hurt, pain, and anguish and, sometimes, physical abuse;

- Isolation and exclusion; and,

- Divisiveness in society.

*Racism is harmful to our society's health. It has hidden social and economic costs.*

II. **"I will concede that racism still exists."**

- Some still use the erroneous concept of "race" to exclude people and to justify inequality, supremacy, domination and persecution.

- We still have rules, regulations, policies, and practices that exclude, limit, and discriminate against those who do not belong to the traditional, dominant group and that judges them and their abilities, and their cultures as inferior.

- No particular group "owns" racism. It exists in all groups.

III. **"I will not yield to pressures to discriminate."**

- I will be a positive role model with my family and among my peers and friends.

- I will value and use the strengths that our society has because of people's differences.

IV. **"I will unlearn my own prejudices."**

- I acknowledge this will be difficult because I have learned them from people around me since early childhood, and we tend to see what we expect or want to see in others.

- I will determine how deep my prejudices are:

  -Were my ancestors steeped in traditions of prejudice?

  - Do I express prejudice through ethnic jokes, slurs, epithets, and by   stereotyping people?

  - Do I identify with groups, which think they gain from acts of discrimination?

- I will understand my emotions and those of victims of racism.

- I will recognize that different does not mean "better" or "worse", but simply different.

- I will break down barriers that make me uncomfortable about behavior and ideas of those who are different from me.  I will develop closer, continuous contact and interact with them.

- I will not fear equal-status competition.  People who are different from me are not an economic threat to me.

- I will become better informed, acquire new insights, make critical judgments, and grow in my understanding of the world.

- I will develop more positive behavior towards members of all ethno-cultural groups.

## V. "I will work towards an 'inclusive' society."

- I will move through the stages of (a) tolerance, (b) acceptance, (c) respect, and, (d) inclusion, to affirmation, where I will advocate and celebrate the diversity and inclusion of all mankind.

- If I do not act, helplessness and victimization will continue and my silence will be interpreted as approval of racism.

- I will help to eliminate racism because it is my responsibility, and that of all people. http://veritas.mzkor.org.

This final statement should be our final challenge. The responsibility to dismantle the ugly wall of racism is **my responsibility** and the responsibility of all people. Particularly those who confess Jesus Christ, as their Savior and Lord can do nothing else but work towards this end. In Luke 6:46 Jesus asked what might be called the most embarrassing question in the Bible: **Why call ye me Lord, Lord, and do not the things that I say?** What exactly has the Lord said? That, we are to love one another as he has loved us.

It is by this example that all men will know that we are indeed His disciples. I admonish you to get busy today and take down the wall of separation in society in general, and in the church in particular, one brick at a time. Every time you intentionally act with kindness, compassion, and respect towards someone of another race or ethnic heritage, you have taken another brick out of the wall. Let us get busy, we have a lot of work to do, but together we **can** succeed.

# APPENDIX A

## SLAVERY AND RELIGION IN AMERICA: A TIME LINE
## 1440-1866

1440's Portuguese begin to capture Africans off the coast of Mauritania and the Senfambia region.

1619 First Africans are brought to English colonies, in particular to Jamestown, Virginia.

1626 The Dutch discovered New Amsterdam. Eleven Africans, all indentured servants, are among the settlers.

1638 The New England Slave trade begins in Boston Massachusetts.

1641 Jonathan Winthrop records first documented baptism of a slave in New England.

1660 Charles II of England urges the Council for Foreign Plantations to Christianize slaves.

1661 Black Codes give statutory recognition to the institution of slavery in colonial Virginia. (Up to this point Africans were indentured servants like other White settlers).

1664 The English take New Amsterdam and rename it New York.

1667 Virginia Assembly passes a law denying that baptism grants worldly freedom to slaves.

1680's Colonial governors in North America are instructed by England to convert slaves and Native Americans to Christianity.

1681  Philadelphia is founded.

1688 Members of the Society of Friends (Quakers) protest slavery in Germantown, Pennsylvania.

1693 Society of Negroes is founded in Boston, Massachusetts.

1694 A group of ministers attempt to persuade the court of Massachusetts to pass a bill permitting slaveholders to retain baptized slaves.

1700's Many North American slaveholder's fear that Christianize their slaves will lead to rebellion.

1701 Society for the Propagation of the Gospel in Foreign Parts is established by the Church of England to send missionaries to the slaves in the North American colonies.

1706 Puritan leader Cotton Mather publishes *The Negro Christianized,* arguing that blacks are indeed human.  He writes, "Man Thy Negro is thy Neighbor."

1707 Isaac Watts publishes *Hymns and Spiritual Songs.*

1712 Slave insurrection in New York City.

1730-1824 The Ursuline nuns of New Orleans concentrate on a mission to black Catholics of the area.

1734 The Great Awakening begins in Massachusetts.  This movement spreads to other areas, encouraging new religious fervor among both blacks and whites.  This movement encourages blacks to join the Methodist and Baptist Churches.

1750's-early 1800's Black preachers minister to free and enslaved blacks.  Small, independent, black congregations begin to emerge in the south.

1758 Probably the first recorded black congregation is organized on the plantation of William Byurd in Mecklenburg, Virginia. It is a Baptist congregation.

1773-1775 The Silver Bluff Baptist Church in Silver Bluff, South Carolina is organized. This is the first separate black church in the United States and is lead by George Liel and David George.

1775 American Revolution (War of Independence) (1775-1783) begins.

1775 A group of Quakers organize the first Abolitionist Society of Philadelphia.

1776 Declaration of Independence.

1777 Slavery is abolished in Vermont

1778 Virginia prohibits external slave trade.

1780 Pennsylvania passes a law that allows for the gradual abolition of slavery.

1780-1810 Almost as many slaves are brought into the United States as had been brought in over the previous 160 years.

1783 War for Independence ends.

1783 Slavery abolished in Massachusetts

1784 Richard Allen and Absalom Jones are first black men to be granted licenses to preach.

1784 "The Christmas Conference" of the Methodist Church passes a resolution against slave holding.

1786 There are 1,890 of a total of 18,791 Methodists who are black.

1786 Richard Allen and Absalom Jones establish the Free African Society in Philadelphia.  This is a response to the need to create a place of worship, social welfare and community for free blacks in the area.  Similar societies soon emerge in other cities.

1787 George Liel, an ex-slave from Georgia, brings the Baptist Church to Jamaica thus becoming the very first American foreign missionary.

1787 Constitutional Convention

1788 Andrew Bryan, a slave, is ordained as a Baptist minister. Bryan gains his freedom when his master dies and becomes the minister of the First African American Baptist Church of Savannah with a congregation of more than 500.

1790 The number of Black Methodists increases to 11,682.

1791The Bill of Rights is added to the Constitution.

1793 An approximated 18,000 or 19,000 of a total of 73,417 Baptists are black.

1794 Absalom Jones becomes pastor of St. Thomas' African Episcopal Church organized on July 12th of that year.  St. Thomas is received into the Episcopal Church on October 12, 1794.

1794 Richard Allen founds Bethel Church for free blacks to worship with dignity.

1797 The number of black Methodists increases to 12,215. Most of these black members are in Maryland, Virginia, and North Carolina.

1799 Second Great Awakening begins with the Cane Ridge camp meeting. The meeting takes place in Kentucky and embraces African Americans. Many slaves are converted to Christianity.

1800 Gabriel's Rebellion is attempted in Richmond, Virginia. Gabriel, called the Black Sampson, uses Old Testament themes as an inspiration to rise up against slavery. Slave revolts in South Carolina, North Carolina, Georgia, Louisiana and Mississippi follow.

1800 The state of Virginia passes a law forbidding African Americans to assemble between sunset and sunrise for religious worship or instruction.

1800 The Great Awakening moves to the frontier.

1801 John Chavis, a "free Negro," is appointed by the Presbyterian General Assembly to work in Virginia and North Carolina to serve as a missionary to other African Americans.

1805 The North Joy Street African Baptist Church of Boston is organized.

1807 The African Union Church, the earliest black Methodist Church, is incorporated in Wilmington, Delaware.

1812 War of 1812 begins.

1812 "Free Negro" and Baptist preacher Joseph Willis forms Louisiana's first Baptist Church at Bayou Chicot. He serves as pastor and helps other Baptist churches in the area.

1814 African Methodist Episcopal Church forms in Philadelphia.

1816 Several African Methodist churches meet at Bethel church in Philadelphia in April and form the African Methodist Episcopal Church.

1818 Louisiana Baptist Association forms, Joseph Willis serves as the Association's first moderator.

1821 The African Methodist Episcopal Zion Church is organized on June 21$^{st}$. AME Zion forms a new denomination with members from New Haven, Philadelphia and Long Island.

1822 Denmark Vesey, a Methodist and a former slave to Captain Joseph Vesey, leads a slave insurrection in South Carolina. Vesey and his men are arrested before they have a chance to put their plan into action.

1827 First African American newspaper, *Freedom's Journal,* begins publication in New York.

1829 David Walker publishes and the first edition of his *Appeal to the Coloured Citizens of the World,* and distributes the work to African Americans in the south. This revolutionary literature warns against the work of white plantation missionaries.

1830 Second Great Awakening ends

1830's-1840's there is increased concern among white churchmen about the religious well being of slaves in the south. This concern leads to plantation missions.

1830-1880 The two Marie Laveaus, mother and daughter, lead voodoo cults in New Orleans.

1831 Nat Turner, a Baptist slave preacher, leads a revolt in Southampton County Virginia, killing at least 57 whites.

1838 Presbyterian Church divides over slavery.

1844 Methodist Church divides over slavery.

1852 Harriet Beecher Stow's *Uncle Tom's Cabin* is published.

1852   Josiah Priest publishes *Bible Defense of Slavery.*

1856 Booker T. Washington is born in Franklin County, Virginia, on April 5th. Washington later becomes a leader in the educational, social and political realms of African American life.

1857 On March 6, 1857 the Supreme Court decides that an African American cannot be a citizen of the United States and has no rights of citizenship.

1860 Abraham Lincoln is elected the 16th President on November 6, 1860.

1861 Civil War begins

1862 Slavery is abolished in the District of Colombia.

1863 The Emancipation Proclamation takes effect as of January 1st legally freeing slaves in areas of the South in rebellion.

1865 On January 31, 1865 Congress approves the Thirteenth Amendment outlawing slavery in the United States.

1865 Civil War ends

1865 President Abraham Lincoln is assassinated.

# BIBLIOGRAPHY

Ajayi, J.F.A. and Crowder, Michael (Ed.). (1973). History of West Africa. New York. Colombia University Press.

Ahlstrom, Sydney E. (1972). A Religious History of the American People. New Haven: Yale University Press.

Allen, Richard. (1833). The Life and Times of the Rt. Rev. Richard Allen. Philadelphia: Martin and Boston Publishers.

Andrews, Joyce. (1993). Bible Legacy of the Black Race. Nashville: Winston-Derek Publishers.

Anyike, James C. (1994). Historical Christianity African Centered. Chicago: Popular Truth Inc. Publishers.

Atiya, Aziz S. (1968). History of Eastern Christianity. South Bend: University of Notre Dame Publishers.

Augustine, Aurelious. (1960). The Confessions of Saint Augustine. Garden City:Doubleday and Company Inc.

Bartleman, Frank. (1925). Azusa Street. Plainfield: Bridge Publishers Inc.

Blascoe, Joanne C. (1993). A Narrative of the Proceedings of the Black People during the late Awful Calamity in Philadelphia in the year 1793 with Richard Allen and Absalom Jones. Missouri. Independence National Historical Park Publishers.

Bragg, George (1904). Afro-American Church Work and Workers. Baltimore: Church Advocate Press.

Bragg, George. (1922). <u>History of the Afro-American Group of the Episcopal Church.</u> Baltimore: Church Advocate Press.

Burkett, Randall K. (1978)   <u>Black Apostles.</u> Boston:  G.K. Hall Co.

Clarke, John Henrik (1993). <u>African People in World History</u>

Davis, J. D. (1924). <u>Davis Dictionary of the Bible,</u> Fourth Edition. Michigan: Baker Book House.

East, J. E. (1965). <u>Lotte Carey, Pioneer Missionary.</u> Washington D.C.; Baptist Foreign Missionary Convention.

Edwards, John H. (1997). <u>The Episcopal Church and the Black Man in the United States.</u> (unpublished) McQuire Theological College.

Felder, Cain Hope. (1991). <u>Stony The Road We Trod.</u> Minneapolis: Fortress Press.

Felder, Cain Hope (Ed.). (1992). <u>The Original African Heritage Study Bible.</u>  Nashville: Winston-Derek Publishers.

Finkenbine, Roy. (1997). <u>Sources of the African-American Past.</u> New York: Longman Publishers USA.

Fitts, Leroy. (1985). <u>A History of Black Baptists.</u> Boston: Broadman Press.

Fitts, Leroy. (1978). <u>Lotte Carey: First Black Missionary To Africa.</u> Valley Forge, PA: Judson Press.

Gibbs, Nancy. (1999). "The Surprise Blessings of Reform." Time Magazine Publishers.

Gurley, Ralph R. (1835). <u>The Life of Jehudi Ashmun, Late Colonial Agent of Liberia.</u> New York: Greenwood Press Inc.

Harmon, Nolan. (1974). <u>Encyclopedia of World Methodism,</u> Volume II.Nashville, TN: United Methodist Publishing House.

Hayden, J. Carleton. (1988). <u>From Holly to Turner: Black Bishops in theAmerican Succession.</u> (Unpublished Paper].

Hyatt, Edward. (1996). <u>Two thousand Years of Charismatic Christianity.</u> Hyatt International Ministries Publishers.

Isichi, Elizabeth. (1995). <u>A Histoy of Christianity in Africa.</u> Grand Rapids, Michigan: William B. Eerdsman Publishers

Jacobs, Sylvia M. <u>Black Americans and the Missionary Movement.</u> Westport: Greenwood Press.

Johnson, John L. (1994). <u>The Black Biblical</u> Heritage Nashville: Winston-Derek Publishers.

Johnson, Paul. (1977). <u>A History of Christianity.</u> New York: Atheneum Publishers.

Johnson, Julian Ramsses. (1994). <u>The Garden of Eden.</u> Nashville: James C. Winston Publishing Company

Kane, J. Herbert (1978). <u>A Concise History of the Christian World Mission</u> Grand Rapids: Baker Book House

Koestler, Arthur (1976). <u>The Thirteenth Tribe.</u> London: Hutchinson &Co. Publishers.

Lauer, Robert (1998). <u>Social Problems and the Quality of Life</u> Boston: McGraw-Hill Co.

Malcioin, Jose V. (1978). <u>How the Hebrews Became Jews.</u> New York: U.B. Productions

Martin, Sandy D. (1989) <u>Black Baptists and African Missions.</u> Macon: Mercer University Press

Newman, Burkett. (1978) <u>Black Apostles</u>. Boston: G.K. Hall and Company

Payne, Daniel A. (1969). <u>History of the African Methodist Episcopal Church.</u> New York: Arno Press

Payne, Robert. (1966). <u>The Christian Centuries.</u> New York: W. W. Norton and Company.

<u>Pentecostal Evangel Magazine,</u> (April 8, 1956). How Pentecost Came to Los Angeles: An Eyewitness Account of the Momentous Events of the Year 1906.

Raboteau, Albert J. (1980). <u>Slave Religion; the "Invisible Institution" in the Antebellum South.</u> New York: Oxford University Press.

Readers Digest. (1974). <u>Great People of the Bible and How They Lived.</u> Pleasantville: The Readers Digest Association, Inc.

Readers Digest. (1994). <u>Who's Who in the Bible .</u> Pleasantville: The Readers Digest Association, Inc.

Richards, Lawrence O. (1987). <u>The Teachers Commentary.</u> Wheaton: Scripture Press Publishers.

Sanders, J. Oswald. (1994). <u>Spiritual Leadership.</u> Chicago: Moody Press.

Schaff, Philip. (1910). <u>History of the Christian Church Volume II; Ante-Nicene Christianity AD 100-325.</u> Grand Rapids: Eerdmans Publishing Company.

Sernett, Milton C. (1985). <u>African-American Religious History; a Documentary Witness</u>. Durham, North Carolina: Duke University Press.

Southern, Eileen. (1983). <u>The Music of Black Americans: A History.</u> New York: W. W. Norton and Company.

Stewart, Jeffrey C. (1996). <u>1001 Things Everyone Should Know About African American History.</u> New York: Doubleday Publishers.

<u>The Encyclopedia Britanica,</u> (1878). Ninth Edition, Volume III.

<u>The Encyclopedia of World Methodism Vol. II,</u> (1974). Nashville: United Methodist Publishing House.

Trulson, Reid. (1993). The Black Missionaries. Article from HIS Magazine. Downers Grove: Inter Varsity Press.(pp.10-12).

Usery, Glenn and Keener, (1996). <u>Black Man's Religion.</u> Downers Grove: Intervarsity Press Inc.

West, Cornell. (1988). <u>Prophetic Fragments.</u> Grand Rapids, Michigan: William B. Eerdsman Publishing.

Wiersbe, Warren W. (1991). <u>The Integrity Crisis.</u> Nashville: Thomas Nelson Publishers.

Whitelaw, Thomas. (1978). <u>The Preachers Homiletical Commentary,</u> Volume 25.Grand Rapids, Michigan: Baker Book House.

Whinston, W. (1981). <u>The Life and Works of Flavius Josephus.</u>

Wilmore, Gayraud S. (1966). <u>Black Religion and Black Radicalism; an Interpretation of Religious History of Afro-American People.</u> Maryknoll: Orbis Books.

Williams, Ethel L. (1972). <u>Afro-American Religious Studies.</u> Metuchen, N.J. The Scarecrow Press, Inc.

Williams, JL. (1996). <u>What the Bible Teaches About Race.</u> Burlington: New Directions Publishers.

Young, Josiah U. (1986). <u>Black and African Theologies.</u> New York: Orbis Books